LARSON'S BOOK OF ROCK

LARSON'S BOOK OF

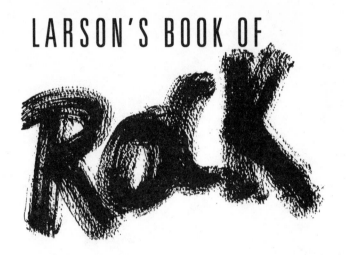

BOB LARSON

Tyndale House
Publishers, Inc.
Wheaton, Illinois

Readers may write to the author at the following address:

Bob Larson
P. O. Box 36480
Denver, CO 80236

This book is an expanded, updated version of *Rock,*
copyright 1980, 1982 by Bob Larson.

First printing, November 1987

Library of Congress Catalog Card Number 87-50994
ISBN 0-8423-5687-8
Copyright 1987 by Bob Larson

CONTENTS

ONE
THE MAIN COURSE WAS ME

I should have known the moment we got in the car that I was in for it. The teenager driving me to a Sunday luncheon engagement turned the radio to his favorite rock station. It was blaring at full volume the heaviest sounds he could find. We were headed for his parents' home, and the worst was yet to come.

I don't often accept private dining invitations because of my demanding schedule. Another reason is my waistline. Good physical conditioning is important to me. It would be pointless jogging my usual three miles a day, then eating three sumptuous meals.

But I need not have worried about the caloric content of this meal. The main course on the menu was me. I had not been invited to eat, but to be eaten.

It was a long, noisy drive to the house. Conversation was impossible over the raucous radio. No one said a word. The airwaves were under the control of David Lee Roth and Motley Crue.

I enjoy popular music. After all, music was my life before I became a Christian. As a professional entertainer, I was immersed in the pop music of my day. I wrote it, sang it, and played it in the early days of rock 'n' roll. Our songs may have sometimes been suggestive, but we never dreamed of WASP's sadomasochistic fantasies or the demonic overtones of Black Sabbath.

I still like a song with good rhythm. Andrés Segovia's interpretation of guitar playing is not the only style I appreciate. But I draw the line when lyrics explore the obscene and profane, and entertainers glorify the perverse and forbidden. That's where I say, "No!"

I was ready to say it now. After leaving the solemnity of a worship service, I was unprepared to hear my driver's favorite rock group sing of salacious sex.

Perhaps I had it coming. My outspoken views on the morally questionable quality of much rock music were well-known to my escort. Maybe this teenage boy was so used to being condemned for the music he listened to that he assumed I had been summoned as a spiritual gunslinger for his parents. He expected me to cram down his throat all their cultural hang-ups. So he was going to get me first.

It was working!

Parents, put yourself in my place. How would you like being locked in your teenager's room for an hour listening to all of his albums? I was in the backseat of a car being chauffeured to a state of nervous anxiety. An easy listening music aficionado might have gone berserk.

I thought we'd never reach the house, where I anticipated peace and quiet. If I had known what was coming, I might have preferred enduring the car radio.

The feast set before us was worthy of a king—or a condemned man being granted his last request. Conversation was pleasant and casual. I was seated with both parents on my left and the teenage driver directly opposite. The atmosphere was slightly tense, but I dismissed it as apprehension about having a new guest at dinner.

I was wrong. It soon became obvious this meal had been arranged to resolve a longstanding parent-child confrontation. About halfway through the meal, the mother folded her arms. Leaning back in her chair, she nonchalantly posed a question. Her acting skills would never have won her an Academy Award.

"Mr. Larson," she began, her formal tone exposing her real intentions, "don't you think that when parents tell their children not to listen to certain kinds of music, they should obey?"

Her teenage son slowly slid down in his chair. He knew it was coming, but the question still embarrassed him. Food suddenly became unpalatable. He drew endless designs with his fork in the mashed potatoes during the ensuing silence.

Mom waited with confident expectation. After all, I spoke against the evils of rock music, and she had invited me to side with her in the continuing confrontation with her son. Wouldn't I reply with an emphatic "Yes!" and put her wayward child in his place once and for all?

I paused for what must have seemed an eternity to both of them. But I needed Solomon's wisdom, and it wasn't immediately forthcoming. I decided to emulate the strategy of Jesus. When the Pharisees asked him a question, he usually posed one to them in return. "Answer mine and I'll answer yours," he would say.

"Please answer a question for me first," I said to the mother. "Do you love your son?"

She was stunned—and offended.

How dare I put her on the spot? Guests were supposed to be more polite. She wanted endorsement, not harassment. She concealed her dislike with the same thespian abilities that had failed to hide her previously expressed hostility.

"What do you mean?" she asked. "I brought him into the world, didn't I? I cook his meals and provide for him. He's supposed to honor and obey me."

"You're not answering my question," I insisted.

Gradually, the intent of my inquiry hit home. Her body relaxed, and she hung her head.

"Yes," she answered. "I do love my son."

"Well, then," I probed further, "when was the last time you told him?"

Tears welled in her eyes. She had invited me there to put her son on the spot. Instead, *she* was in the hot seat.

I glanced at her son, who barely suppressed his glee at seeing Mom on the defensive for a change. But he shouldn't have gloated so readily. He was about to be put on the spot.

"Do you love your parents?" I asked him.

He hung his head. He didn't enjoy having the shoe on his own foot.

I barely heard the yes he muttered under his breath, but his answer was audible enough to warrant my next question.

"When was the last time you told them?"

Through the mist that formed in his eyes, he looked across the table at his parents. Almost simultaneously, the three of them burst into tears. I sat quietly, at ease with the long-neglected display of affection between parents and child.

When the crying and expressions of sorrow and regret subsided, I carried my point further.

"Do you know what the problem is in this home? No communication across the generational barrier," I said. "I've never been to your house, but I can guess what happens most evenings. You eat a hurried meal, then depart in different directions. You head for the TV," I said, looking at Mom and Dad, "for entertainment that pleases you. Then," I went on, referring to the son, "you go to your bedroom and turn on the stereo."

I directed my attention back to the parents. "A little later that beat from the music pounding through the ceiling gets on your nerves. So you yell up the stairs, 'Turn that junk down!' "

Mother and Father nodded in agreement.

"Then," I said to the son, "knowing how much it irritates them, you turn it up louder."

The son grinned with embarrassed acknowledgment.

"After a little longer," I added, "the music irritates you even more, so you yell up the stairs again."

"And you," I said to the son who was getting more and more fidgety, "turn it up all the louder."

My analysis was nearly complete.

"The problem in this home is not the kind of music your son listens to. The real dilemma is that you live in separate worlds, screaming insults and injuries. The only time you talk is to tell each other how objectionable the other's life-style is."

Before leaving, we all joined hands around the table for a time of prayer to heal the scars of a wounded home.

I didn't know at the time, but the teenage son had never accepted Christ as his Savior. That Sunday evening he was the first to step forward and request prayer for salvation at the conclusion of the service.

This is not a unique story. Many homes face similar situations. I constantly encounter parents who are alarmed at their children's musical tastes. For some, the mere sound of rock is objectionable, so loud and noisy and unlike *their* music.

Parents may be vaguely aware of some dangers in the rock scene, but their concern is seldom expressed constructively. It tends to be high-handed or uptight, sometimes downright overbearing. That attitude only compounds the problem. If your child has absorbed rebellious attitudes fostered by rock stars' immorality, imposing musical censorship will only make matters worse.

But there is a way out of this dilemma. As parents, you can

establish Christ-honoring musical norms for your family. Teenagers can be taught discretion in musical tastes. They can learn to please the Lord as well as Mom and Dad. It won't be an easy confrontation, but your home's spiritual future may depend upon it.

TWO
WHAT'S LOVE GOT TO DO WITH IT?

In 1954, Cleveland disc jockey Alan Freed was searching for a term to describe teenagers' wild response to a new musical fad. Violent riots and sexual hysteria accompanied concerts by Chuck Berry and Gene Vincent. Millions of female eyes were glued to the groin of Elvis. A musical—and sexual—revolution was in full swing.

Freed found his phrase in a ghetto expression referring to fornication: rock 'n' roll. The name stuck, and the beat went on. But rock lyrics eventually explored fringes of lyrical pornography Freed never dreamed of.

Adults, who are naive about the sexually explicit content of today's pop hits, say, "So what? Things were bad in our day, too. Didn't girls swoon over Sinatra? And what about Cole Porter's 'Let's Do It' "?

It's true that Porter slyly suggested imitating the birds and bees, but he quickly qualified the innuendo: "Let's do it—let's fall in love."

Many of today's popular songs aren't that ambiguous.

Love means sex to most contemporary rock composers. If meaningful relationships are referred to at all, they usually are described as fruitless or pointlessly painful. Most rock expresses love in a single dimension—desire. Lust is the motivation, conquest the goal.

This is reflected in song titles. The old hack about "crooning a tune in the month of June under the moon" gave way to "Let's

Spend the Night Together" in the 1960s, "I Want to Kiss You All Over" in the 1970s, and "What's Love Got to Do with It?" in the 1980s. The Beach Boys' 1960s hit "Wouldn't It Be Nice?" referred to the anticipation of being married to the desired girl, but if that title were used for a song today, it definitely wouldn't be about marital bliss.

Many song titles in the last several years seem to extol premarital and extramarital sex. Consider Loverboy's "Hot Girls in Love" and Marvin Gaye's "Sexual Healing." Ray Parker, Jr.'s "The Other Woman" and Whitney Houston's "Saving All My Love for You" made adultery sound delightful. Consider also "Do That to Me One More Time," "Let's Get Physical," and "One Night Love Affair."

Album titles aren't exactly mild, either. Some that come to mind are Wham's *Make It Big,* Pat Benatar's *Seven the Hard Way,* Tina Turner's *Break Every Rule,* David Lee Roth's *Eat 'Em and Smile,* Ratt's *Dancing Undercover,* and Madonna's *Like a Virgin.*

Some album jacket designs are pornographic. The parent who presumes his son would never read *Playboy* is in for a shock when he thumbs through the average teenager's stack of records. Duran Duran's single "Skin Trade" was originally released with the cover showing a close-up shot of a women's bare behind. A spokesman for Capitol Records insisted the cover was "perfectly tasteful." Circum-venting criticism, the American version of "Skin Trade" featured a cherry red cover, though the Canadian version had the shot of the bare behind. John Taylor of the group responded to the controversy by admitting the song was about the selling power of sex. Taylor declared, "I'm kind of pleased about all of this in a way. Now I'm 100 percent certain that what we're talking about in the song is true."[1]

But the titles and covers are only the tip of the iceberg. It is the lyrics that make the sex-is-everything message so clear. In the tune "Knockin' at Your Back Door," the band Deep Purple made it plain they weren't speaking about the entrance to a building. The singer described the "log" in his pocket and his attempts to seduce "sweet Nancy" so he could "get inside her pantry." Motley Crue's "Looks That Kill" refers to a young girl's genitalia as a "motor" she keeps clean, even though she's "a number thirteen." Steve Miller's "Abracadabra" described his lover's lingerie and appearance as "black panties with an angel's face."

A national controversy erupted over Sheena Easton's lyrics in

"Sugar Walls," which invited her lover to spend a night "inside my sugar walls." Sheena admitted that the tune, written by Prince, was erotic. She said, "It is sexually suggestive, and it raises the imagination. That is what art is supposed to do."[2]

Rock lyrics leave little to the imagination. Intimate acts are thoroughly explained to teenagers. Cyndi Lauper sang about masturbation in her hit "She Bop," wailing about being unable to "stop messin'" with her genitalia, which she called her "danger zone."

Male performers provide most sexist lyrics. In his song, "Little Miss Dangerous," Ted Nugent described a young lady who is on fire for sex and "burns all night long." ZZ Top, in their album *Eliminator,* sang about a lover's legs and her proficiency in knowing "how to use them." Night Ranger in the tune "Touch of Madness" described learning about love "in the back of a Chevrolet." Another singer speaks of the venereal disease he collected on a trip as a souvenir he can't declare at customs. "Only the Good Die Young" by Billy Joel lamented that Catholic girls stay virginal too long.

Doug Feiger, of the defunct group the Knack, explained the philosophy of the group's songs this way: "We've been accused of writing about women as sex objects, and I don't think that's so bad. Everyone wants to be a desirable sex object. Everyone. It's a human thing."[3] To prove their point, Feiger and friends sang of teenage love as a "sticky sweet romance" and a lustful young man who wants to get "inside her pants."

The days of Pat Boone and Doris Day are long gone. Teens don't want performers who are sweet and demure. Formerly innocent-imaged Olivia Newton-John released an album called "Soul Kiss" containing a tune "Culture Shock," which *People* magazine described as "a musical tribute to a ménage à trois."[4] Another tune, "Overnight Observation," is about a doctor seducing a woman patient. *People* observed, "If Olivia's career keeps going this way, just about the only thing she'll be able to do next is to record an album of duets with Dr. Ruth."[5]

Sex for the sake of satisfaction is all Eddie Money described in his song "Take Me Home Tonight." Describing his body as an automobile, he pleaded with his lover to "find the keys and turn the engine on." All he wanted was to be taken "home tonight . . . I don't want to let you go till you see the light . . . I hate to sleep alone."

Vinnie Vincent, former guitar player for KISS, commented on their songs "Shoot You Full of Love" and "I Want to Be Your Victim." He admitted, "The stuff in the album should be X-rated. It's really pornographic. A song like 'I Want to Be Your Victim' is the ultimate rock 'n' roll bondage number."[6]

If such explicit sexual descriptions shock you, hang on! Wait until you decipher the code language by which erotic lyrical images are conveyed. Automotive terms like "engine," "motor," and "machine" are all employed as sexual euphemisms. Teenagers who understand such language are cynically amused because Mom and Dad's moral objections to rock's lyrics have been cleverly circumvented. No wonder one rock periodical called explicit lyrics "prophylactic rock,"[7] and the music industry refers to sex-oriented tunes as "masturbatory rock."

With such thematic exploitation, parents understandably worry about what comes next. The answer is, "It gets worse!" The examples cited here aren't the worst ones. Some songs are so lewd that the lyrics can't be printed without demoting this book to pornography. Having explored every moral limit to excite and titillate, some rock composers have included the subject of sadomasochism, inflicting physical pain for sexual pleasure. The Rolling Stones' "Beast of Burden" and John Cougar Mellencamp's "Hurt So Good" are examples of excursions into formerly forbidden territory. (There is still some sanity around. Hall and Oates, not noted for keeping sexual content out of their songs, did record "I Can't Go for That," a musical refusal to participate in sadomasochism.)

The performers themselves almost arrogantly proclaim that they are selling sex. David Coverdale of the group Whitesnake says that their album titles like *Slide It In* and *Love Hunter* are about sex. Coverdale says, "Isn't sex what rock 'n' roll is all about?"[8] Nikki Sixx of the group Motley Crue says, "We're intellectuals on a crotch level."[9] Composer/producer/artist Johnny Bristol says, "Sex is where it's at in music . . . and I like it."[10] Singer John Oates agrees, declaring that rock 'n' roll is "99 percent sex."[11]

"I've always thought that the main ingredients in rock are sex, really good stage shows, and really sassy music. Sex and sass, I really think that's where it's at," claims Debbie Harry, formerly lead singer with the group Blondie.[12] Her lead guitarist and lover, Chris Stein, agrees. "Everybody takes it for granted [that] rock and roll is synonymous with sex."[13]

This isn't too surprising, since rock artists are not known for their high moral character.

A rock periodical ran a series of interviews with rock stars who detailed their personal sex habits. One well-known female singer revealed she uses the rhythm method with multiple partners. The Tubes' Fee Waybill explained that he always checks the birth control method used by fifteen-year-olds before seducing them.[14]

David Krebs, former manager of Aerosmith, explains, "When you're in a certain frame of mind, particularly sexually oriented, there's nothing better than rock and roll. Because that's where most of the performers are at."[15] Speaking about their album *Girls, Girls, Girls,* Motley Crue's bassist Nikki Sixx claimed that the album focused on "girls, motorcycles, sex, and drugs—all the traditional rock things."[16]

A sexy image seems to make stars more attractive. Donna Summer (now a professed Christian) is an example of stardom achieved by sexual emphasis. Her first disco hit, "Love to Love You Baby," was a seventeen-minute vinyl aphrodisiac. It recorded her moaning the title phrase repeatedly to the accompaniment of rapturous groans and murmurs in a marathon of twenty-two orgasms.

Some rock stars' blatant eroticism is referred to as the WPS—the "Wet Panty Syndrome." Referring to singer Bryan Adams, a rock periodical observed, "There's still some question of whether the most blatantly fanatical of his followers are more impressed by the tightness of his act or the tightness of his pants."[17] The rock video phenomenon has made a star's appearance even more significant than before, for youth can watch such blatantly sexual performers as David Lee Roth in their own living rooms. He and such erotic performers as Billy Idol and Madonna can now be not only heard, but watched, twenty-four hours a day.

The very names of certain rock groups reek of sex. Steely Dan is named after a male dildo. 10 C.C. based their name on being one cubic centimeter more than the average male seminal emission. You'd probably rather not read such things in a family-oriented book. But remember, these are the groups your children listen to, and they probably already know this information. You need not fear this book; rather, fear the rock stars that teens idolize as omnipotent oracles speaking the truth about life and love.

Sex is so important to selling records that a special preview house was set up in Los Angeles to test new songs demographically. As each number was played, listeners turned dials to register their response. Some seats were equipped with "basal skin response sensors" that measure involuntary spasms of the nervous system. The programmers admitted they were searching for songs producing an orgasmic effect.[18]

Who's to blame for such irresponsible exploitation? Who produces and promotes such warped ideas to pollute young minds? Certainly not teenagers themselves. Mercenary adults run the major record companies. Driven by greed and avarice, they care nothing about your child's morals and will descend to any depth to arouse teenage sexual curiosity.

Not everyone is willing to let the companies and producers off the hook. Jesse Jackson has suggested that record companies accept some responsibility for the high rate of black teenage pregnancies.[19] George David Weiss, president of the Song Writers Guild, declared, "Where lyrics once used innuendos, they are now overt. Where lyrics were once artfully suggestive, they are now blatantly explicit. Where lyrics once extolled tenderness and love relationships, they now glorify violence and loveless sex. Have we forgotten the airwaves belong to the people? I submit that the only sensible course of action is industry-wide self-restraint."[20]

Columnist George Will wrote in *Newsweek,* "Rock music has become a plague of messages about sexual promiscuity, incest, sadomasochism, satanism, and misogyny. There is a connection between self-restraint and shame. An individual incapable of shame and embarrassment is probably incapable of the governance of the self. A public incapable of shame and embarrassment about public vulgarity is unsuited to self-government."

David Gergen, writing in *U.S. News and World Report,* said, "The difference between music of yesterday and that of today is the leap one makes from swimsuits in *Sports Illustrated* to the centerfolds of *Hustler.*"

Shocked though you may be, you probably must admit you know little of rock music and are unaware that sexually explicit albums are on public display throughout your city. Worse, they may be in your own home. Adult ignorance contributes to the proliferation of rock pornography marketed for your children.

"Now that I know, what can I do about it?" you ask.

Keep reading! Help lies ahead.

NOTES
1. *Rolling Stone,* March 26, 1987, p. 10.   2. *USA Today,* October 25, 1985,
p. 2D.   3. *Rolling Stone,* October 18, 1987, p. 37.   4. *People,* November 1985.
5. Ibid.   6. *Hit Parader,* February 28, 1986, p. 28.   7. *Rolling Stone,* February 9,
1987, p. 100.   8. *Hit Parader,* July 1986, p. 61.   9. *Denver Post,* April 28, 1985,
p. 2D.   10. *Rolling Stone,* April 5, 1987, p. 23.   11. *Rolling Stone,* April 21, 1977,
p. 15.   12. *Hit Parader,* September 1979, p. 31.   13. *People,* May 21, 1979.
14. *Circus,* February 20, 1976, p. 24.   15. *Circus,* October 17, 1978, p. 34.
16. *Hit Parader,* May 1987, p. 41.   17. *Circus,* September 30, 1983, p. 22.
18. *Denver Post,* April 28, 1985, p. 61.   19. *Billboard,* June 29, 1985, p. 10.
20. *Billboard,* June 29, 1985, p. 10.

THREE
PORN ROCK—
HOW DO YOU RATE IT?

The scene was a Senate hearing room in Washington. The occasion was a meeting of the Senate Commerce Committee. Rock star Frank Zappa was there with his lawyer and a copy of the First Amendment. John Denver was there too, comparing censorship of rock lyrics to practices of the Nazis. Dee Snyder of Twisted Sister was there, claiming he was a Christian while admitting the obscene meaning of the letters SMF on his album *Stay Hungry*.

Susan Baker, wife of the Secretary of the Treasury James Baker, initiated the debate over porn rock after hearing her seven-year-old daughter listening to Madonna sing "Like a Virgin." The appalled Mrs. Baker stated, "The issue affects my family. I really believe that the escalation of violence and sexuality is a form of child abuse."[1] Influential Washington wife Pam Howard started listening seriously to the lyrics played in her aerobics class. Tipper Gore, wife of Senator Albert Gore of Tennessee, expressed outrage at the lyrics of rock hits.

When the Senate met, Senator Ernest Hollings of South Carolina listened to the likes of Blackie Lawless of WASP and Vince Neil of Motley Crue and proclaimed that their songs were "outrageous filth." Hollings declared, "The framers of the First Amendment never considered broadcast airwaves that would pipe this stuff willy-nilly into homes."[2] Senator Hollings also coined the term "porn rock."

Senator Paula Hawkins of Florida showed portions of the Van

Halen video "Hot for Teacher" and Twisted Sister's "We're Not Gonna Take It Anymore." Then she held up for TV cameras a copy of a WASP album showing the lead singer sporting a buzz saw between his legs and a four-letter sexual expletive which she hesitantly quoted to the assembly.

The proceedings irritated Senator James Exon of Nebraska. Senator Hawkins responded to him with, "No one has the right to poison our children with these lyrics."

There was a reaction in the rock camp, of course. Rocker Frank Zappa claimed the Washington wives behind the antiporn-rock campaign were "the wives of Big Brother." Zappa stated, "Fundamentalism is not a state religion. I want my children to grow up in a country where they can think what they want to think and be what they want to be and not what someone in government makes them to be." Before the day was over, Zappa had called the Washington wives "cultural terrorists" with "antisexual pseudo-Christian legislative fervor."[3] Dee Snyder compared rock videos' violence to Roadrunner cartoons, implying that neither the videos nor the cartoons are taken seriously.

When questioned about his opposition to what the Washington wives were doing, Frank Zappa declared, "There's nothing wrong with scatology." Zappa, whose songs are noted for obscenity, stated that obscene language supplies metaphors that are comprehensible by a marginally literate person, if that is the audience one is trying to reach. Arguing for freedom to use street language, Zappa said, "You're not going to address them in the language of Euripides."[4]

But the Washington wives of the Parents Music Resource Center (PMRC) were not put off by such protests. After the Senate hearings they started stomping the media trail, warning America about the group Judas Priest advocating oral sex at gunpoint, Motley Crue describing quickie sex in an elevator, and Sheena Easton singing about genital arousal in her song "Sugar Walls." The wives pointed out that, between the seventh and twelfth grades, teens listen to an estimated ten thousand hours of rock music—the same amount of time they spend in twelve years of school.[5]

PMRC concerns were echoed by others. The National Council of Churches concluded that music videos figure significantly in antisocial behavior.[6] The National Education Association estimated that five thousand teenage suicides each year were linked to depression fueled by fatalistic lyrics.[7] And when Richard Ramirez was charged with sixteen "night stalker" murders on the West Coast, it was found that he had been obsessed with AC/DC's album *Highway to Hell*.

The secular press began to take notice of porn rock. *U.S. News and World Report* commented that some psychologists were theorizing that rock music is "creating false puberty among kids in the fourth, fifth, and sixth grades." The same issue quoted one fan of Cyndi Lauper as saying, "Life ends at twenty. What is there after that?"[8]

Journalists around the country began to express concern. Columnist William Safire commented on what he called rock music's "explicit glorification of kinky sex." Safire stated, "Some well-adjusted kids laugh it off, but the values of enough are profoundly affected. They wonder what's wrong with doing what seems to be universally accepted."[9]

A study conducted by a New York marketing research firm indicated that three-quarters of all American adults agree there should be a rating system for records. Of the one thousand adults surveyed, 80 percent believed that lyrics should be visible on the album or tape package, and 78 percent believed that "the record industry should take steps to regulate itself."[10]

The Washington wives and others who shared their concerns had abandoned their proposal that records carry ratings (V for violent content, X for sexually explicit lyrics, and O for occult references). But they did win a victory of sorts. Twenty-two major record labels endorsed the proposal (made by the Recording Industry Association of America) that companies should print warning labels on albums or print lyrics if the songs contained explicit references to sex or violence. Cassettes, which have no space for lyrics on the covers, would have the words "See LP for lyrics."[11] However, no provision was made for enforcing this, and each company was left to decide which of its products, if any, would require warning labels.

CBS Records did institute a policy on sexually explicit, violent, and drug-related lyrics. Employees were told in a memo, "If you believe that a future release contains such [objectionable] lyrics, you should notify . . . the appropriate department head. If a lyric's warning is contractually permissible, then the inscription 'Explicit Lyrics—Parental Advisory' should be placed on the recordings containing such lyrics. The inscription may be placed by sticking or imprinting."[12]

Stores began to participate in the antiporn movement. The chain of Wal-Mart stores agreed not to sell several albums by some hard rock stars, including groups such as Black Sabbath, Judas Priest, Motley Crue, Ozzy Osbourne, and AC/DC. Wal-Mart also pulled thirty-two teen and rock magazine titles from their shelves, a decision that affected eight hundred stores. Magazines pulled included such popular titles as *Rolling Stone, Hit Parader,* and *Teen Beat*. Executives at various record companies, aware of the Wal-Mart move, said they saw the product deletions as symptomatic of an ongoing sensitivity in some consumer quarters.[13] Christopher Finan of Media Coalition, a group of publishers, booksellers, and book distributors, called the Wal-Mart move "a particularly good example of how censorship works."[14] A more sane response came from Bob Guccione, Jr., publisher of *Spin:* "It's not censorship in the strictest sense. . . . Wal-Mart has the right to put what they want in their stores."[15]

Some governments also began to take action. The city council of Cleveland passed a resolution urging radio stations not to play songs with blatantly obscene lyrics. San Antonio, Texas, passed an ordinance that barred unescorted children thirteen and younger from performances in city-owned facilities where lyrics or simulation depict bestiality, sadistic or masochistic sex, sex with a child or corpse, exhibitionism, rape or incest, or anal copulation. (The Texas Civil Liberties Union said it would test the constitutionality of the city law. Gara LaMarsche, executive director of the group, said, "It's going to be almost impossible to determine how old a child is. Are they going to bring their report cards or birth certificates?"[16])

President Reagan entered the fray by declaring, "I don't believe our founding fathers ever intended the rights of pornographers to take precedence over the rights of parents and the violent malevolent to be given free reign to prey upon our children."[17]

But opposition to warning labels continued. A group called the Musical Majority protested, claiming that labeling and ratings were censorship pure and simple. Among its members were Tina Turner, Bruce Springsteen, Dolly Parton, Olivia Newton-John, and Lionel Ritchie. Chairman of the group, Danny Goldberg, said, "Wives of politicians are interpreting song lyrics and trying to impose their personal interpretations on every artist and everyone in the U.S.A. . . . There is a country where committees tell people what to sing . . . it's called the Soviet Union."[18] (For the record, not all artists are so opposed to rating records and printing warning labels. Mike Love of the Beach Boys donated five thousand dollars to the Parents Music Resource Center to help wage war on porn rock.[19])

Frank Zappa offered to place his own warning sticker on record albums. He suggested that it would refer to "material which a truly free society would neither fear nor repress." Zappa said he wanted to use the sticker to assure listeners the recordings wouldn't "cause eternal torment in a place where the guy with the horns and the pointed stick conducts his business."[20] Clearly, Zappa and other rock artists have no time for the warning labels.

Criticisms of the warning labels have come from other quarters. A spokesman for the National Association of Recording Merchandisers (NARM), Russ Solomon, expressed concern that warning stickers would "probably increase the sales for albums with racy lyrics." (There may be some truth to this—consider how many R-rated movies achieve popularity and how few G-rated movies are produced nowadays.) Solomon went on to say, "I have felt from the beginning that it's not an issue. If something is so patently objectionable, then it will seem to be non-broadcastable and won't be recorded in the first place."[21] Given the salacious nature of many rock songs, Solomon is obviously wrong. Songs with offensive sexual content are released every day.

The board of directors of NARM went on record as "unanimously opposed" to the establishment of a rating system or warning labels on records. NARM defended the right of free expression and called for voluntary efforts to "assure that industry product remains within the boundaries of good taste." In opposing the ratings or a warning sticker, the NARM board concluded that "the problem which would be created by efforts to review and assess the more than twenty-five thousand new songs which are written annually would far outweigh the benefits to be gained. Such an effort might not only stifle creativity and freedom of expression, but also might well deprive the general public of songs that would otherwise be appropriate."

NARM also declared that the number of controversial songs is "a very small fraction" of the total released each year. The board said that a warning system would "only encourage interest on the part of young people to purchase recordings containing warning notices" and that "to put store clerks or store managers in the position of determining when and under what circumstances such recordings should be displayed or sold would be an intolerable burden."[22]

The International Council of Shopping Centers (ICSC) also formally opposed any sort of censorship. The ICSC was concerned that shopping malls could urge record stores to pull records off shelves in response to community protests about sexually explicit or violent lyrics. The ICSC public relations director said, "If there was a big hue or cry, management would probably try to convince the retailer to go another way, to pursue an alternative." The ICSC worried that landlords might put language into leases that could cancel store space for actions that would "cause controversy in the community" or be "detrimental to the mall."[23]

Opponents of record rating killed a Maryland law that would have imposed a thousand-dollar fine and a one-year sentence on anyone convicted of selling to a minor any record, tape, or compact disc with lyrical content or cover art judged to be pornographic. Frank Zappa was there to fight the measure. He told members of a Maryland Senate committee, "lyrics do not harm you" and that "no sound that comes out of your mouth will send you to hell."[24] Zappa also told the committee, "To say rock music is a major cause of antisocial behavior is not supported by science. . . . Take a look at normal kids who listen to it every day. They don't commit suicide. They don't commit murder. They grow up. In some cases, they grow up to be legislators."[25]

After a trial period during which the record industry was given an opportunity to comply voluntarily with the warning label agreement, the Parents Music Resource Center declared it was not entirely pleased by efforts of the Recording Industry Association of America. In a press statement, the PMRC accused the RIAA of "blatantly ignoring, sidestepping, or mocking the agreement." PMRC cited fifteen albums that should have carried warning labels or printed lyrics under the agreement. The PMRC said the albums contained a total of twenty-five offending songs. Sally Nevius, president of the PMRC, and Ann Kahn, president of the National PTA, stressed that what they want is a standardization of the "Explicit Lyrics—Parental Guidance" warning label, with similar placement and size on albums.[26]

The PMRC and NPTA cited Metallica's "Master of Puppets" and Metal Church's "The Dark" as examples that should have received warning labels. The song "In Your Face" by Fishbone was singled out for having a warning only one-sixteenth of an inch high and buried in the back cover's artwork. The PMRC said, "If an album with explicit lyric content carries the logo of a company which is part of the agreement, even though that company may only be participating in the distribution of that album, it should carry the consumer information."[27]

A major test of anti-obscenity measures against explicit records occurred in the case of the Dead Kennedys' album *Frankenchrist*. At issue was a poster in the album by Swiss artist H. R. Guger showing ten sets of male and female genitals engaged in sexual intercourse. The Los Angeles city attorney's office filed misdemeanor criminal charges against Jello Biafra, the group's lead singer. A municipal judge ruled that Biafra was not protected by the First Amendment and could be held responsible for the sale of the poster. The incident occurred after a mother complained that her teenage daughter was able to buy the album and poster at a music store as a gift for her eleven-year-old brother. California has a law banning distribution of harmful materials to juveniles.[28]

Biafra didn't deny that the painting, entitled "Penis Landscape," is offensive. In fact, a sarcastic warning sticker was included on the album's shrink-wrap. Biafra argued, "Only a sicko would be turned on pruriently by the poster. It has literary, scientific, political, and artistic value."[29]

Such a statement would be laughable if there was not so much at stake. God's most beautiful act of intimacy, sexual union, is consistently degraded in so much rock music, and those who degrade it defend their endeavors by saying they have literary and artistic value. Such twisted logic is a warning to parents who have underestimated the power and perversion of porn rock.

This whole controversy has made it obvious that purveyors of porn, whether it is in the form of books, films, or record albums, like to appeal to the First Amendment. Knowing that most Americans prefer to think of themselves as free people in a free society, the producers and performers who record and sell porn immediately begin screaming "Hold on to your freedom!" as soon as concerned parents express their desire to warn buyers that the material is sexually explicit. Clearly the porn producers are protecting their own interests. They are not too interested, obviously, in protecting freedom in America unless *freedom* means the right to sell salacious material to impressionable youth. The producers and artists may mouth words about maintaining a free society, but they have no interest in supporting the morals that are essential to a free and stable nation.

The controversy is by no means resolved, nor is it likely to be.

Record companies will continue to produce records and tapes with sexually explicit songs. *Jet* magazine reported that one record store owner claimed that out of four hundred releases per month, ten or less had warning labels.[30] Even if all offensive materials carried warning labels, children and teens would continue to buy them. The burden of censorship does not lie with the recording industry nor with the PMRC nor with any group, but with parents. While the efforts of the PMRC and other like-minded groups are to be applauded, keep in mind that you, the parent, are responsible for offensive material being in your home. You can't control what your child hears while away from home, but you can listen carefully to the records he owns and observe the visual messages on the album covers. And you can learn more about the artists, which is why this book includes a glossary of contemporary performers.

NOTES
1. *Time*, September 30, 1985, p. 70.   2. *Music News*, pp. 9-11, 15, 62, 64-66.
3. Ibid.   4. *USA Today*, October 18, 1985, p. 7A.   5. Parents Music Resource
Center Letter, 300 Metropolitan Square, 655 15th St., N.W., Washington, D.C.
20005.   6. *USA Today*, October 11, 1985, p. 10A.   7. *U.S. News and World Report*,
October 28, 1985, p. 46.   8. Ibid.   9. *DMN*, October 14, 1985.   10. *Rolling
Stone*, August 21, 1986, p. 26.   11. *USA Today*, November 4, 1985, p. 5D.
12. *Rolling Stone*, no date.   13. *Billboard*, August 2, 1986, pp. 1, 77.   14. *Seventeen*,
January 1987, p. 86.   15. Ibid.   16. *Fort Worth Star Telegram*, November 6, 1985,
p. 32A.   17. *USA Today*, November 11, 1985, p. 10A.   18. Ibid.   19. *Music News*,
pp. 9-11, 15, 62, 64-66.   20. *Billboard*, September 14, 1985, p. 100.   21. *Billboard*,
November 16, 1985, p. 75.   22. *Billboard*, November 2, 1985, pp. 3, 80.
23. *Billboard*, December 7, 1985, p. 7.   24. *Billboard*, March 29, 1986,
pp. 3, 81.   25. Ibid.   26. *Billboard*, December 20, 1986, p. 3.   27. Ibid.
28. *Rocky Mountain News*, February 14, 1987, p. 74.   29. *Spin*, September 1986,
p. 24.   30. *Jet*, July 14, 1986, p. 56.

FOUR

A CHIP OFF THE OLD BLOCK

"Your son acts just like you," Mom says.

Whether the mother is frustrated or admiring, the result is usually the same: Dad flushes with pride. He wants his son to be like him. But for some parents, that flush turns to a blush. The Gay Revolution is upon us, and the sons we wanted to be football heroes discover they would rather frequent gay bars.

Unless you've been living in Outer Mongolia, you know only too well that today's child is threatened with unprecedented homosexual influences. Keeping your child straight is no longer an assured outcome of child-rearing, but a goal to be adamantly protected.

I have yet to meet the most liberal parent who wanted his child to become a homosexual. A child reflects parental values. Your reputation is affected by your child's behavior. He can bring to your senior years either fulfillment or heartache. He is a chip off your block, and undoubtedly you pray for his future to be untainted by perversion. Even if his sexual behavior did not affect your reputation in any way, you would know that the gay life-style is an ongoing exercise in frustration, emotional ruin, and, with the coming of AIDS, a downright threat to life. And it is against the will of God.

It probably disturbs you as a parent when civic and church leaders speak favorably about homosexuality. As public men and women and role models, they influence younger generations who revere them. But the real influences on style and morality are entertainment stars, who have a profound impact upon youthful sexual identity.

With homosexuals coming out of the closet to stage frontal assaults on society's morals, it was inevitable that rock music would deal with gay life-styles as a cultural reflection.

Rock interest in homosexuality is not new. Several years ago, the Kinks took a lyrical fling at sexual ambiguity in a song called "Lola," describing a homosexual who "walked like a woman and talked like a man."

In like manner, Frank Zappa and the Mothers of Invention were exploring bisexual themes as early as the mid-sixties. They wore women's clothing for the cover of one album.

Various artists have reflected homosexuality in their appearance. Before his death, Keith Moon of The Who appeared in public wearing women's clothing. When the gay-rock trend first hit in the early 1970s, the Dolls, a New York City rock band, sported lead singer David Johansen wearing skintight trousers and platform heels and bass guitarist Arthur Kane in pink tights. For years, Mick Jagger of the Rolling Stones has worn mascara to further flaunt his reported bisexuality.

Among the best-known entertainers exploiting gay rock are Lou Reed and David Bowie. Reed, now married, was for a while a member of the Velvet Underground, a rock act produced by the late self-proclaimed homosexual artist Andy Warhol. He began his career singing about bleak visions of a drug-dominated nightmare world. On one of his earliest albums, *Transformer,* Reed was pictured on the jacket in high heels, panty hose, rouge, and mascara. Some of the songs included were "Make-up," a tune about dolling up and coming out of the closets "into the streets," and "Good-night Ladies," which tells of a perfumed homosexual's lonely Saturday nights. In another song entitled "Vicious," he describes hitting his lover with a stick during sexual relations.

David Bowie is a talented British singer/composer/guitarist who, in the past, boasted of his bisexuality in interviews and songs. His ex-wife is an admitted lesbian. He rose to fame over a decade ago, sporting orange hair and laced high-heeled boots, moving effeminately to a rock beat. Bowie portrayed acts of copulation on stage with other males while singing homosexual songs like "Queen Bitch." In spite of such perverted extravagance, Bowie became a major superstar. His concerts are sellouts wherever he goes.

The group Culture Club, extremely popular in the early 1980s, had several major song hits. Boy George, the lead singer, often plucked his eyebrows, wore make-up, and dressed in shapeless smocks and a porkpie hat, claiming that he and the group represented all cultures and sexes. His long-term relationship with another group member became widely known. On a sellout world tour in 1984, Boy George flaunted his bisexuality by announcing during the concerts that he would "like to sleep with each member of the audience individually." The cover of the album *Waking Up with the House on Fire* showed George with heavy makeup and a mane of luxurious red hair. (For more information on Culture Club, see the glossary in this book.)

Elton John, pop music's talented pianist with the enormous glasses, has been fairly outspoken about his sexual deviations. Though married for a time, he was involved for many years with his lyricist, Bernie Taupin. John has been popular for well over a decade and shows no sign of decline. Interestingly, his 1986 song "Nikita" seems to have been addressed to a Russian male lover. Though the song's video showed Nikita as a woman, Nikita is almost always a man's name in Russian. (Elton is discussed in more detail in this book's glossary.)

While some pop superstars manage to maintain a large following in the population at large, some artists cater to a smaller audience. A gay label, Olivia Records, marketed lesbian albums with songs like "Gay and Proud" and "Women Loving Women." These productions have not achieved much of a following.

Still, many performers do try to cater to gays. Before their professional demise, the female trio Labelle appealed to an adoring gay following. As singer Nona Hendryx put it, "I like appealing to both men and women. I don't limit myself. I'm all sexes."[1]

Singer Cindy Bullens says, "I definitely feel I am bisexual. I have never been one sex in my whole life."[2]

Straight artists like Daryl Hall and John Oates felt obliged to attract gay crowds. For one album, they posed for the cover shot in heavy makeup. Hall replies, "The idea of sex with a man doesn't turn me off. I had lots of strange experiences with older boys between when I was four to fourteen."[3] The video for the Hall and Oates song "Possession Obsession" contains some obvious homosexual scenes. Olivia Newton-John's video for "Physical" had a humorous—and perverse—punch line: the handsome, muscular young men at Olivia's spa turned out to be gay, and they walked out arm in arm, leaving Olivia with an overweight (but heterosexual) patron.

The British rock group Queen has included several songs on their albums that seem to indicate a predeliction for homosexuality or bisexuality. "Sweet Lady" and "Now I'm Here" playfully switch genders in the lyrics, so the singer seems to be singing suggestively to both men and women. As Queen's appeal widened in the early 1980s, lead singer Freddie Mercury changed his style, looking more like the "butch" homosexual with short-cropped hair, neatly trimmed mustache, and body shirt. He has given up the pink leotards and doesn't sing in a falsetto so often now, but even the group's name seems to attest to sexual ambivalence. (*Queen* is still a widely used term for an effeminate homosexual man.)

Todd Rundgren leapt on the bandwagon by adding varicolored hues to his shoulder-length locks. A sadomasochistic group, the Cycle Sluts, strutted onstage in corsets and black lingerie.

Some gay groups and singers have achieved limited success. Jobriath was heralded as the ultimate gay star. He declared, "I'm a true fairy. I'm selling sex."[4] But the public didn't buy his paeans to homosexual love.

Steve Grossman was heralded as the "Bob Dylan of the gay movement." Mercury Records made him the first gay minstrel promoted by a major label with the release of "Caravan Tonight." Singer Tom Robinson combined homosexuality and politics. His band's logo featured a clenched fist, and the record sleeves of his albums contained information about a gay switchboard advising young homosexuals on how to come out of the closet. Robinson's odes to perversion included "Let My People Be" and "Glad to Be Gay."

David Bowie helped launch the careers of artists like Eno, Iggy (once arrested for female impersonation), and Wayne County. The outrageous County appeared in full drag with a purple wig and rhinestone-studded bathrobe. He declared, "I always wanted to be a homecoming queen. I was such an unlucky little girl." He typified gay rock's depravity by comments like, "Jesus Christ was a strange boy himself."[5] County's songs included "It Takes a Man Like Me to Like a Woman Like Me."

County was outdone only by the absurdity of British star Alex Harvey, who proclaimed, "Homosexuality is a good thing. It stops the population from getting any bigger."[6]

For awhile, Mick Ronson was David Bowie's lead guitarist.

Bowie sometimes got on his knees to play Ronson's guitar with his tongue with obvious phallic overtones. When asked how he liked such antics, Ronson replied, "I took my bisexual image seriously. I didn't like it at first, but then you get used to it. With so many people around you being bisexual, you get used to it for yourself."[7]

Gay rock groups had to go a long way to top Alice Cooper's outrages. Claiming to be the reincarnation of a seventeenth-century witch, Alice began his career by appearing on stage dressed in women's clothing and wearing heavy mascara.

In the 1970s, Alice Cooper performances wedded perversion and violence as he chopped a lifelike doll into pieces, made love to a writhing snake, and hung himself on a gallows. In spite of such contrivances, Alice was asked to lecture at the Eastman School of Music in Rochester, New York. His subject was "the art of writing popular music."

Not all of Alice's fans responded positively to the Alice Cooper act. Once a man charged the stage during a concert and tried to kill Alice by hitting Cooper over the head with a beer bottle. On another occasion, an M-80 bomb exploded onstage. Once his drummer found blood flowing down his back, and discovered he had been stabbed by darts hurled from the audience.

Still, youth can't help but notice that some rock artists like David Bowie appear to live rich, successful, and happy lives, a powerful endorsement of sexual ambivalence. No matter how well you've trained your child to disdain sexual perversion, the incessant onslaught takes its toll. Your child may know homosexuality is wrong, but how long can he fend off his rock idol's insistence that gay is good?

Parents, wake up! The storm troopers for gay liberation have attacked with guitars in hand. Fortunately, few rock artists are actually gay, and gay-rock trends have subsided in the eighties. But those still condoning homosexuality represent a disproportionate share of society at large. This imbalanced inclination can produce subliminal disaster for the young person who favors the music of such artists.

Sadly, in some homes the son isn't a chip off his dad's block. Rather, he's been rewhittled to more closely resemble the likes of David Bowie. If you don't want that to happen in your home, this book is designed to help you.

NOTES
1. *Rolling Stone,* July 3, 1975, p. 43. 2. *Rolling Stone,* July 5, 1979, p. 23.
3. *Rolling Stone,* April 21, 1977, p. 15. 4. Ibid. 5. *Hit Parader,* June 19, 1975,
p. 71. 6. *Circus,* July 1975. 7. *Circus,* August 1975, p. 70.

F I V E
WHERE DID WE GO WRONG?

Knock, knock.

You try to rouse your husband. "Honey, wake up. There's someone at the door."

You fumble for the light switch. It's midnight. Who would come at this hour? It couldn't be your daughter. She said she'd be staying overnight with a friend.

Finally, both of you awaken and head for the front door. You open it. There stands your daughter and a police officer. What could she have done wrong? She can't even look at you. She hangs her head in shame.

There's a stunned silence. Then the officer says, "I've just picked up your daughter driving under the influence of drugs. We'll have to take her in and book her. Would you like to come along?"

In ten seconds, your world disintegrates. Other parents have problems with children who take drugs. But not you. Yours is a Christian home. You raised your daughter in church and Sunday school. This is a nightmare.

The police officer is waiting for an answer.

"Yes, we'll come with you. Won't you come in and have a seat while we get ready?"

The two of you don't look at each other while you dress. But covert glances reveal the same question on both of your faces: "Where did we go wrong?"

All the plans and hopes for your daughter have been crushed.

She'll bear a stigma the rest of her life, and perhaps a jail record. Her future—and yours—is a big question mark. The family reputation has been tarnished. People will regard you as failed parents.

As all these fears crash down upon you, one question must be answered: "Where did we go wrong?"

Before you sink further into self-condemnation, you must realize that probing your past parental role is probably pointless. Chances are you tried to raise your child properly. But there's one reason for your daughter's disaster you may never discern. You may falsely assume that your training and advice were the major influence in your child's life. But I've got news for you. Someone else occupied her ears and mind more. Someone communicates more with her in one day than you do in a week. And that someone isn't a teacher, her pastor, or a schoolmate.

Stop and think for a moment. What is she most exposed to daily? Music!

You may have done your best as a parent, but it's hard to counter that constant absorption of prodrug attitudes prevalent in today's music. It's all there in the songs and lyrics and the public image of the rock stars whose records your child listens to. It may be hard to accept, but face it. How that entertainer feels about doing dope may influence your child more than your warnings against substance abuse.

What kind of drug philosophy does the rock generation support? The rise of the hippie movement in the late 1960s encouraged a rash of songs with persuasive attitudes toward drugs. Some songs openly advocated turning on, while others simply condoned.

It can be argued that merely mentioning drugs in a song doesn't convey approval. But casual discussion of drug usage elevates the subject to a degree of familiarity and acceptance. Advertisers know that the desirability of a product to consumers is directly proportionate to the frequency of its mention. Drug users know this too.

In the 1960s, drug-rock songs declared that youth should take a "Magic Carpet Ride" or a "Journey to the Center of Your Mind." The Beatles sang, "I get high with a little help from my friends." That the latter song became a pop standard illustrates how our culture is desensitized to off-the-cuff drug references.

At a recent International Music Conference, the spokesman for a major record industry advertising firm stated: "Record companies and music publishers have earned many millions of dollars from extolling the virtues of drugs. Would one turn out phonograph records extolling the virtues of forceful rape, armed robbery, or kidnapping? The answer, I think, for many companies is yes, as long as there is money in it and they don't go to jail." A prominent rock manager stated, "No matter what anyone tells you, drugs will always be part of the rock scene."[1]

Rock critic Robert Forbes appraised rock and drugs this way: "Drugs are a necessary ingredient for many rock musicians. It is almost impossible to sustain the frantic pace, ungodly hours, and inhuman energy without resorting to some kind of drug. The rock musician thrives on the periphery of that high and uses it as a crutch to hold his position, audience, and individuality."[2]

Cocaine is openly snorted at many recording studios and is an accepted celebratory toast when signing contracts. Many entertainers insist that turning on is no big deal. Being arrested for drug violations is fashionable in some rock circles, certainly not rare. Consequently, if your child attends concerts of such artists and is later offered a dose of dope, he probably will view it as something his rock idol has used and enjoyed.

Tragically, your child's possible drug conviction won't be shrugged off as easily as that of wealthy rock stars represented by high-priced attorneys. A major disc jockey put it this way: "Most of the artists I talked to refused to be anticocaine because they use it."[3]

You may warn your child against the dangers of drugs, but listen to what his rock heroes tell him:

"We were sitting, passing around a joint—a doobie—so we called ourselves the Doobie Brothers"—Tom Johnston of the defunct Doobie Brothers.[4]

"I'm in the music business for the sex and narcotics"—Glenn Frey of the now disbanded Eagles.[5]

"We avoid all hard drugs like cocaine, although we do smoke marijuana now and again"—the Bee Gees.[6]

"I smoke a lot of pot . . . that doesn't necessarily mean I'm high"—Jerry Garcia.[7]

A list of prominent rock artists who have openly admitted drug usage would be too lengthy to recount. Some more notable examples of rock stars include Jimmy Buffett, David Crosby, Stephen Stills, Leon Russell, Joe Cocker, Eric Clapton, and Johnny Winter. Keith Richards of the Rolling Stones was charged with heroin possession. Some years ago, Mick Jagger of the Stones was presented with a silverplated snuff box for cocaine at a birthday party in Madison Square Garden.

The saddest commentary on the rock drug scene is the destruction of those drug zealots who once glorified drugs. Rock stars live in a world of fast cars and large sums of money, an unreal existence of overindulgence brought on by wealth and stardom. Many burn out in their prime.

Jimi Hendrix ushered in the drug-death syndrome when he suffocated in a pool of his own vomit after an overdose. Within two weeks, Janis Joplin and Jim Morrison followed him to similar fates. Brian Jones of the Stones drowned while high in his private swimming pool.

In his book *Only the Good Die Young,* rock writer Robert Duncan discusses twenty rock heros who met untimely deaths. In an appendix of his book entitled "Rock and Roll Heaven," he lists sixty-seven rock stars who died, most of them from drug abuse. Among them were James Honeyman-Scott of the Pretenders (cocaine), Janis Joplin (heroin), Tommy Bolin of Deep Purple (heroin), Sid Vicious of the Sex Pistols (heroin), session blues guitarist Michael Bloomfield (heroin), Led Zeppelin drummer John Bonham (alcohol), and AC/DC lead singer Bon Scott (alcohol).

Drug overdoses also caused the deaths of Al Wilson of Canned Heat, Gram Parsons, Gary Thain of Uriah Heep, Vinnie Taylor of Sha Na Na, Keith Moon of The Who, and Lowell George of Little Feat. Rock king Elvis Presley's body was like a human pincushion at the time of his death in 1977. Presley's drug use had become such an obsessive habit that there was almost no space left on his needle-scarred body to make new injections. The fact that most of the drugs involved in his death were prescribed made no difference. Both legal and illegal drugs can cause dependency and, in many instances, death.

Casual drug abuse didn't cause these tragedies. In most instances, death was due to multiple overdoses of one or more drugs including pot, cocaine, barbiturates, and alcohol.

Sly Stone came close to death but managed to survive repeated nose operations for cocaine snorting along with run-ins with angel dust.

Perhaps most frightening is the nonchalant attitudes of many rock stars toward drug usage. "I take drugs to get in an unpleasant frame of mind and then try to find a catharsis for it. It's a self-sacrifice," brags David Weiss of the New Wave band Was (Was Not).[8] When he was arrested in Japan for possession of 7.7 ounces of marijuana, Paul McCartney shrugged off the incident by saying, "Marijuana isn't as dangerous as some people make it."[9] After stating numerous times that he was against drug use, Boy George of Culture Club was found out to be a heroin addict.

But there are dissenters. Steven Tyler of Aerosmith, for example, has encouraged his band to do anticrack benefits. Tyler says, "I haven't done any cocaine in a year. . . . It's the devil's drug. It will kill you."[10] The Thompson Twins' album *Here's to Future Days* included the song "Don't Mess with Dr. Dream," an antidrug anthem.

These names probably mean little to most parents, but your teenager knows these people as top performers in the rock world. Known to nearly every youth in the land, these are the idols who told your child to turn on in the first place.

Rock musicians, who use high-paid attorneys to beat their drug raps and spend thousands on operations and detoxification programs to patch up their bodies, owe their popularity to the patronage of young fans who have financed such high living. More responsible conduct and public statements against drugs are the least to ask from those in control of impressionable young minds.

For every rock star done in by dope, another comes along to claim the cause of substance abuse. But what of the dead? Who purchased their records and supported their drug habits? Who yelled for another encore and pushed the pressures of stardom beyond endurance? Their fans, that's who. Maybe your own son or daughter.

What killed these undisciplined musicians—the drugs, or the demands of the fans who drove them to destruction? It's a point worth making to your child before he buys another album of an artist devoted to dope.

Encouraging your child to boycott the music of artists who advocate or use drugs could save this generation a lot of misery. It could also save your family from that midnight knock on the door.

Beyond monitoring the music your child listens to, consider the importance of your own life-style. Kids are always watching their parents, and they notice when Mom and Dad use alcohol, muscle relaxers, or tranquilizers to cope with stress. It is unlikely that you are using any illegal substances, but do you ever find that chemicals help you "unwind" or face a stressful situation? If you do, be sure your child has noticed.

An occasional use of a prescribed muscle relaxer is no crime, but be aware that our whole culture is oriented toward seeking pleasure and avoiding pain. If your own habits convey the message that drugs are useful for coping with stress and making life more pleasant, you are helping your child toward drug use. Cocaine may be a far cry from a once-a-week valium, but the best thing you can do in your home is to show that mature people can have a good time—and cope with the bad times—without resorting to drugs and alcohol. To the child who is on the verge of experimenting with drugs, the thing that might push him over the brink is the awareness that Mom and Dad resort to drugs to make life easier.

NOTES
1. *Circus*, April 17, 1979, p. 16.   2. Ibid.   3. *Rolling Stone*, November 22, 1973.   4. *Rolling Stone*, January 4, 1973, p. 16.   5. *People*, June 30, 1975, p. 60.   6. *Circus*, August 3. 1973, p. 38.   7. *Spin*, April 1986, p. 21.   8. *Rolling Stone*, August 20, 1981, p. 10.   9. *Rolling Stone*, March 6, 1980, p. 30.   10. *Hit Parader*, March 1987, p. 25.

S I X

DEPROGRAMMING YOUR CHILD

"Good afternoon, sir," she says, smiling broadly. "My name is Laurie."

The pedestrian is taken aback for a moment. Nobody smiles or stops to speak on a busy city street. What does she want? Before that question can be answered, she pins a bright red carnation on his lapel.

"I represent an organization that feeds starving children in the Third World," she informs the bewildered man. "Could you make a donation to our worthy cause?"

He is intrigued by her fresh smile and pleading look. Who wouldn't trust such an innocent-looking young lady?

He reaches into his pocket and pulls out a dollar bill.

"Don't you have something larger? Babies are dying every day because we don't have enough food to give them."

For a moment he ponders the request. She's right. A dollar sure won't buy much these days. And this young solicitor does look trustworthy.

Screeeeech!

A sedan pulls up to the curb. The doors fly open, and two men jump out. One of them clamps his hand over Laurie's mouth, while the other twists her arm into a hammerlock.

The pedestrian is stunned as he watches Laurie forcibly shoved into the car. The doors slam, and the woman driver speeds away, careening through traffic.

What should he do? Should he run to the nearest policeman?

He could, but it would be pointless. The two men were her father and brother, and the driver was her mother. This was not a kidnap but an abduction. The car is on its way to a motel where a professional deprogrammer waits.

That smiling young lady? She's a member of a religious cult and has forsaken all to follow her guru. The temple she attends owns her worldly possessions and is the controlling force in her life.

Her parents haven't seen her since the day she disappeared a year ago. No letters, no phone calls, nothing. But for a friend who recognized her in this distant city, Laurie might never have been found.

The parents had agonized over the loss of their child, but their guilt was worse. How could this have happened to their daughter?

They read every book about cults they could find. The brainwashing techniques interested them most: "love-bombing," low-protein diets, sensory deprivation, little sleep, and constant indoctrination by cult leaders.

Still, it was hard to believe that such tactics could have so quickly transformed Laurie's beliefs and character. One question had nagged at them those long twelve months. Did something exist in her past that affected her thinking and made her susceptible to cult teachings?

The distraught parents searched everywhere for a clue. They quizzed friends and teachers and consulted Laurie's pastor. They suspected the books she read and every movie she had seen. But they uncovered nothing that could alter her so dramatically.

But the parents overlooked one place in their search: Laurie's bedroom. A stereo sat in one corner. Near it was a huge collection of rock albums.

Her parents never cared for the kind of music Laurie listened to. They dismissed her interest as a passing teenage fad. The philosophy and life-styles of her rock heroes were never scrutinized. Too bad. One look at her favorite records would have uncovered a major culprit in Laurie's conversion to the world of cults. Those vinyl pressings and cardboard jackets were more than mere entertainment. Through them, the religious philosophies of the East were meeting the teenage mind of the West. And in the process, Kipling's dictum, "East is East and West is West, and never the twain shall meet," was being proved wrong.

What records were found in Laurie's library?

On the top of the stack was an early album by the Moody Blues. Its title, *In Search of the Lost Chord*, referred to the mystical concept of a musical chord with supernatural vibrations. If that exact chord can be struck, the listener is said to gain instant enlightenment through a transcendent state.

Inside, the album sleeve pictured a yantra, the visual equivalent of the verbal chant known as the mantra. An explanation provided the Hindu and yogic background of the yantra. While the record is played, the listener is told to stare at the geometric designs and thereby enter an altered state of consciousness. God is declared to be embodied in the very sound of the Hindu Sanskrit word *OM*, the title of one cut from the album.

The rest of Laurie's records reveal a similar vein of Eastern religious viewpoints. An album by the group Yes was entitled *Tales from Topographic Oceans*. The jacket explained that the lyrics were based on Hindu scriptures and were specifically inspired by Paramahansa Yogananda's book, *Autobiography of a Yogi*. The songs of the album were said to reveal "the science of God," including tantric sexual rituals and reincarnation.

Confusion about the oblique lyrics of mystical rock songs is often dispelled by instructions on the album jacket. One example is the Strawbs' record, *Grave New World*, which included a quotation from Buddha and a prayer of praise dedicated to the Egyptian sun god, Ra.

A variety of other rock artists have entertained a serious or flirting interest in Eastern religions. England Dan and John Ford Coley joined Seals and Crofts in promoting the Baha'i faith. Before retiring from entertainment, Seals and Crofts used their concerts to overtly evangelize, and Coley says, "I had a strong Christian background."[1]

One of the more zealous rock artists to espouse transcendental thought was the British star Gary Wright. A follower of Paramahansa Yogananda, he spoke in his hit "Dream Weaver" of traveling to astral planes (out-of-body experiences). He composed the tune while meditating under a pyramid. He acknowledged that before his concerts he performed kriya yoga, a highly spiritistic branch of yoga.

Mike Love of the Beach Boys has ardently promoted Transcendental Meditation and claims to have fasted to the extent he attempted communication with nature and birds. An early devotee of the

Maharishi Mahesh Yogi, Donovan still defends the guru, even though the Beatles eventually rejected the Hindu mystic whom they accused of woman-chasing. With an obvious commitment to Hindu theology, Donovan says, "What the Maharishi laid on us is pretty strong. Truth lies in everybody. If you meditate for years, it trains your mind to become one with the source of thought."[2]

Shawn Phillips, the folk-rock minstrel, advocated self-control through yoga breathing techniques. Felix Cavaliere, the main force behind the Rascals (an early 1970s rock group) also pursued yoga and meditation as taught by Swami Satchidananda. Cavaliere proclaims his spiritual goal is the attainment of union with the universe.

The late John Lennon managed at least one oriental hit, "Instant Karma," based on the Hindu doctrine of cyclical retribution. The king of rock, Elvis Presley, though he had recorded at least one gospel album and always performed one or two gospel songs in his concerts, was interested in Eastern religions before his drug-related death in 1977.

An adamant and well-publicized Hindu advocate is John McLaughlin, guitar virtuoso of the Mahavishnu Orchestra (now disbanded). The very name Mahavishnu (McLaughlin's "spiritual" name) suggests adoration of Vishnu, one of the trinity of major Hindu deities. McLaughlin, who was once into heavy drugs, now lives a life of submission to his guru, the Hindu spiritual master Sri Chinmoy.

During performances, McLaughlin introduced each song by explaining the metaphysical implications of the lyrics. The audience was asked to join in a moment of meditation. His adoration of Chinmoy surpasses most typical guru worship. "I am immersed in him," he explains. "He is a Divine Being. Perfection. Through the grace of Sri Chinmoy, I've become more aware of the real presence of the Supreme Being."[3] Such worship has monetary aspects, and much of Mahavishnu's income was devoted to Chinmoy. As McLaughlin explained, "My guru knows how to spend my money better than I do."

Can such devotion lead to involvement with evil forces? McLaughlin admitted as much when he described the inspiration for his music. He declares, "When I let the spirit play me, it's an intense delight. My role as a musician is to make everyone aware of his own divinity."[4] On another occasion, McLaughlin was more specific regarding the inspiration of his performances. "One night we were playing," he says, "and suddenly the spirit entered into me and I was playing, but it was no longer me playing."[5]

The band, Mahavishnu, gave way to another group called Shakti, the Hindu goddess who supposedly resides at the base of the spine and is released through yoga positions.

McLaughlin is responsible for turning on Carlos Santana, leader of the popular Latin rock group Santana, to Chinmoy. Carlos, who used to dig wine and grass, opted for meditating with candles and a picture of his new guru. He claimed to have increased devotion for Christ (whom McLaughlin believes lives in everybody), but he adopted a Hindu name, Devadip, meaning, "The lamp of the light of the Supreme." Santana said of his new faith, "It was like being born again."[6] He has since professed a personal commitment to Jesus Christ, being truly born again.

After looking through her albums, Laurie's parents might have understood how she could so readily convert to a strange religious cult, for the cult's teachings weren't that strange. Laurie had already encountered their doctrines. What she was being taught at the temple, she had previously absorbed daily in her bedroom.

Laurie's favorite artist was George Harrison. It was through his songs that she became so immersed in the Eastern view of life. Harrison's records are not only a tool of Eastern evangelism, but a significant portion of the proceeds from their sales goes to support the Hare Krishna cult. Airport travelers have been accosted by cult members who solicit for donations in exchange for a copy of *Bhagavad-Gita As It Is*. George Harrison wrote its foreword.

Why has George Harrison so zealously expounded Eastern mysticism? In his days with the Beatles, he turned John, Paul, and Ringo eastward to the Maharishi Mahesh Yogi. Harrison was a practicing Hindu as early as 1967, long before today's assorted gurus and Krishna Consciousness chanters gained popularity. Since the early days of the Maharishi, his faith in Hinduism has grown. Witness his composition, "My Sweet Lord": The song is a prayer of dedication to Lord Krishna, an incarnation of the Hindu godhead and supposedly the central figure in the *Bhagavad-Gita,* probably the best-loved of Hindu sacred writings. The album *All Things Must Pass* was Harrison's first musical solo, a record replete with praise of Hinduism.

To parents who wonder about Harrison's commitment, listen to these words of evangelistic zeal published in a prominent rock periodical: "I realize now that it was the spiritual side of Indian music which attracted me in the first place. Now it is the only reason for living. The only reason for being here is to have full understanding of the spiritual aspects of life. Eastern religion taught me that the ideal is to become one with God through meditation and yoga."

On one occasion, Harrison journeyed to Kali Temple in Calcutta, India. He prostrated himself before the hideous idol of the Hindu goddess of destruction, Kali, and had a replica shipped to his London mansion where it could be worshiped daily. (Kali is depicted as standing on corpses, holding a bloody severed head, and wearing a necklace of human skulls).

One of Laurie's albums by George Harrison was entitled *Living in the Material World*. The cover pictures a hand holding a symbol taken from the *Bhagavad-Gita*. Inside the album, Harrison is shown wearing a clerical collar and sporting a Hindu chant button. An inner sleeve contains another large color picture of Lord Krishna. Most disturbing is the message contained in the songs. "Give Me Love" contains the line "keep me free from birth," a reference to the Hindu attempt to circumvent the reincarnation life cycles. Harrison also sings the Om chant, an utterance that is supposed to be the symbolic expression of the Hindu godhead.

Living in the Material World professes to have recollections of the "Spiritual Sky," referring to memories supporting reincarnation. The prayer in this song is not directed toward a definitive deity but to the Hindu concept of an ambiguous, impersonal god present in all beings (pantheism). Harrison concludes with his hope to get out of this world by "the Lord Sri Krishna's grace, my salvation."

Harrison boldly declares, "I couldn't relate to Christ being the only son of God." In an interview he concluded, "I'm a very poor example of a spiritual person."[7]

His rambling search for something spiritual led him into herbs, acupuncture, and Satya Sai Baba, who claims to be the Christ.

Things seem to have gotten progressively worse for Harrison. The popularity of his music faded in direct proportion to his mystical involvements. His 1980s albums have sold poorly, and he was sued for plagiarizing the melody to "My Sweet Lord," a melody that, according to the courts, Harrison lifted from the sixties' hit "He's So Fine."

Many of Laurie's other albums revealed mystical roots. But that does her parents little good now. It's too late. Perhaps they can deprogram her, but the emotional scars left by this psychologically brutal procedure only augment the trauma of her past in the cult. If only her parents had paid attention to the albums in her room, Laurie's story might have been different.

Maybe it's not too late for your family. A simple check of your child's records may prevent heartache and disaster.

Rock music isn't the only conveyor of Eastern religious thought in our culture. Pantheism invades the philosophy of nearly every person's thinking, from environmentalists to college professors. Mysticism is heralded on television and in the press. Actress and author Shirley MacLaine is probably the best-known propagator of Eastern (and New Age) thought. Rock isn't the only offender, but it is a major one. And, perhaps most dangerously, it's the one least suspected by parents.

"It won't happen to my child!"

Are you sure? That's what parents of scores of shaven-headed ascetics thought. That's what Laurie's parents thought. Before you make the same mistake, it would be wise to check out your child's record library now.

Rock's fascination with mysticism has faded in recent years. Most of the examples above influenced a generation prior to your teenager's peers. But rock continues to serve as an expression of contemporary values that are likely to be antithetical to a Christian worldview. Check out those records before having to deprogram your child from a spiritually alien ideology.

NOTES
1. *Rolling Stone,* April 4, 1977, p. 23.   2. *Rolling Stone,* November 25, 1971.
3. *Rolling Stone,* March 20, 1972, p. 26.   4. *Newsweek,* March 3, 1972, p. 77.
5. *Circus,* April 1972, p. 38.   6. *Rolling Stone,* December 30, 1976, p. 12.
7. *Rolling Stone,* April 19, 1979, p. 74.

S E V E N
SYMPATHY FOR THE DEVIL

"As for me and my house, we will serve the Lord," Joshua declared. To your family, those words are probably a motto in principle, if not in fact.

You take seriously the responsibility to raise your children in fear of the Lord. God holds you accountable for your household's spiritual standards. Knowing that, you carefully guard against any intrusion of evil into your home.

While other families indiscriminately watch television, you closely monitor your children's viewing habits. Every day begins with devotions and ends with prayer. If your son walked into the house with *The Satanic Bible* under his arm, it would go straight into the trash can. If your daughter tried to experiment with a Ouija board in the darkness of her room, you'd stop it immediately.

But are such measures sufficient for a family living in the midst of today's occult explosion? Is it possible that, while you proclaim your house is the Lord's, other gods are extolled under your roof? Is the stereo in your child's room an altar to darkness that dispenses the devil's liturgy?

To some, such suspicions are tainted with fanaticism. You remember the 1950s when the "jungle beat" of rock 'n' roll was reviled by clergy and musicians alike. And have you forgotten that Elvis's twitching pelvis was considered the epitome of vulgarity, and black rhythm and blues was called "heathen"?

But rock is heard everywhere today. You are accompanied by its relentless rhythm in shops and restaurants, on the job, and in the car. Could anything so pervasive be sinister? Aren't popular singers simply declaring the virtues of love, albeit with some vulgarity and profanity?

If that's what you think, take a journey through the world of occult themes in the rock scene. Be prepared for a jolt. Your generation indulged sex and alcohol, but some of today's entertainment heroes have added other vices—satanism and the occult.

The list of entertainers who have ventured into the occult reads like a Who's Who of rock royalty. Elton John's lyricist, Bernie Taupin, once decorated his walls with satanic art and said, "The occult fascinates me."[1] Australian rocker Billy Thorpe released an LP entitled *Children of the Sun,* a concept album about extraterrestrials who closely monitor earthlings. A German band went to the extreme of calling itself Lucifer's Friend and offered fans "devilishly good rock 'n' roll," calling one release "the demonic new album."[2]

Todd Rundgren went from Egyptology to excessive indulgence of pot and the mystical ways of Sufism.[3] His album *Ra* was dedicated to the Egyptian sun god. The $250,000-stage for his band, Utopia, included a twenty-five-foot gold pyramid. Song lyrics were based on Japanese and Egyptian mysticism,[4] and Rundgren believes in astral projection and reincarnation.[5]

Maurice White of Earth, Wind, and Fire confesses involvement in palmistry, astrology, Transcendental Meditation, and UFOs. "It's all oneness, man," he says. "I'm continuing life from Atlantis [the lost land of occultists]. I have seen a couple of ghosts. They don't scare me . . . beings exist in other dimensions."[6] Before going on stage, White, who believes he possesses occult powers from previous incarnations, has the entire group join hands in a circle to tap into a force of "higher powers."[7] The name of the group was chosen to encompass the elements, with "wind" representing their music, and "fire" derived from White's astrological sign, Sagittarius. His faith was initiated by a study of Buddhism resulting from his involvement in the martial arts.[8] The big-selling album *All in All* portrayed Christian and occult symbols as synonymous in authority and intent. Songs included "Serpentine Fire," which is about the spinal life energy centers of yoga taught in Eastern religions.

Foremost rock occultist Ritchie Blackmore, formerly with Deep Purple, split to form his own group, Rainbow, and then rejoined Deep Purple. Blackmore admits he has attended seances "to get closer to God" and sometimes leaves his body (astral projection) to float about the concert hall during performances.[9] He has recorded in a seventeenth-century castle supposedly haunted by a demon, who is a servant of the 4,000-year-old Babylonian god Baal.[10] His interest in occultism inspired such songs as "Yoga for Health," "Stargazer" (about the slave of an Egyptian witch), and "Tarot Woman" (concerning predictions of occult Tarot cards). Known for his temper, violence, and moodiness, Blackmore dresses appropriately in black.

Ritchie changed the spelling of his first name to conform with numerological beliefs. He likes "ghost hunting" and has experienced supernatural demonic manifestations during seances. "Mental hospitals are full of people who are actually possessed by trouble-making spirits," he insists. Of his own spiritualistic involvement he points out, "I must meet a hundred 'witches' a month. The real ones are reluctant to come forward with their stories. You can tell when they're sincere."[11]

Formerly the lead guitarist for the now defunct Led Zeppelin, Jimmy Page runs a close second to Blackmore in occult inclinations. Page once owned an occult bookstore called Equinox and revered the late, infamous British spiritualist, Aleister Crowley. Noted for murders and sexual perversion, Crowley was so evil he renamed himself "The Beast 666."[12] Page bought Crowley's mansion, and he claims to hear chains dragging and footsteps on the stairs.

Shocking? That's nothing compared to the occult involvement of some of the best-known rock and pop performers. Before his death, Jimi Hendrix was deeply involved in the demonic supernatural. He wore a Hopi Indian medicine shirt and said he came from an asteroid belt off the coast of Mars. Jimi claimed to see UFOs filling the skies above the Woodstock rock festival.[13]

Pop singer Phoebe Snow told a chilling story of communications with a Ouija board, which foretold her pregnancy five months in advance. She experienced a variety of poltergeist phenomena, including shaking beds and mirrors and disappearing objects. Although this brush with demons scared her so badly she abandoned the board, she still gives psychic readings and included in one of her albums a song about parapsychology, "My Faith Is Blind."[14]

Another female artist, Joni Mitchell, previously credited her creative impulses to a "male muse" named Art. She said she was married to him and roamed naked with Art on her forty-acre retreat.

Her responsibility to this musical guide was so strong, she declared, that when he called she would forsake lovers and excuse herself from parties.[15]

Stevie Nicks also flirted with the occult. Her hit "Rhiannon," recorded with the group Fleetwood Mac, was about a Welsh witch.[16] A glance at a Fleetwood Mac lyric sheet reveals that most of their songs are published by the Welsh Witch Company. Stevie Nicks has dedicated songs during concerts to "all the witches of the world."

Other popular rock artists whose music has explored occult themes include:

Stevie Wonder—His album *Songs in the Key of Life* was scheduled for release to coincide with his astrological sign, Taurus.[17]

Daryl Hall—Like Jimmy Page, Hall was a follower of Aleister Crowley. An admitted initiate of magic, he claims his song "Winged Bull" is dedicated to the ancient Celtic religion.[18]

Al Jardine—a member of the Beach Boys, Jardine has his astrology charts done to determine previous incarnations.[19]

Jackson Browne—Browne says his song "Rock Me on the Water" has mythological significance and declares, "Reincarnation is a certainty. It's a belief."[20]

Tangerine Dream—This group performed in a thirteenth-century cathedral while smoking pot and urinating on its pillars.

Dr. John—An ordained minister in the Louisiana Church of Witchcraft, Dr. John wears voodoo necklaces.[21]

Meat Loaf—The album *Bat out of Hell* features pictures of demons and tells of a mutant biker who rides out of the pit of hell. Composer Jim Steinman says, "I've always been fascinated by the supernatural and always felt rock was the perfect idiom for it."[22]

Nazareth—Two of their albums, *Hair of the Dog* and *Expect No Mercy,* displayed covers featuring demon manifestations that could have been painted by an artist who had spiritual encounters. Another example of demonic art is found in the representations of Lucifer on Savoy Brown's *Hellbound Train*.

Santana—Their early album *Abraxas* was named after a witch-craft demon.

Uriah Heep—An album entitled *Demons and Wizards* features a variety of occult songs about astral projection, such as "Traveler in Time." A later album called *Abominog* pictured a fanged demon with blood spilling from its mouth.

David Bowie—Bowie purchased a record player to play records

backwards because he believed songs from his *Young Americans* album resembled Tibetan spiritistic chants. At one stage of his career, he reportedly drew pentagrams on his walls and made hexes while candles burned.[23]

Few groups could top the Rolling Stones for displays of blatant interest in evil. One of their early albums was entitled *Their Satanic Majesties Request.* For the cover, they posed as witches. A Richards-Jagger composition, "Sympathy for the Devil," became an unofficial satanic anthem. In this song, Lucifer himself speaks and requests "courtesy" and "sympathy" from all who meet him.

The ultimate Stones embodiment of dark images came on their album *Goat's Head Soup,* part of which was recorded at a Haitian voodoo ritual. Behind the music are heard screams from those who are becoming possessed of evil spirits. One song, "Dancing with Mr. D.," describes a graveyard romp with the devil. A color picture inside the album shows a severed goat's head floating in a boiling cauldron. Surely the Stones are aware that the goat's head is the universal symbol of Satan worship.

The group Sam Hain, a name taken from the Luciferian Lord of the Dead, features what could be called "death rock." Their most recent album is entitled *Unholy Passion.* Rulan Danzig of the group says, "I'm really into skulls and bones and things. We are definitely into the gore scene. We have a slightly different approach to death than most people do. If you don't understand or realize what death is, you won't be able to enjoy life."[24]

The group Venom declares on one of its albums, "We are possessed by all that is evil, the death of your God we demand, we spit at the virgin you worship, and sit at Lord Satan's left hand." Their songs include "In League with Satan," "One Thousand Days in Sodom," and "Live Like an Angel (Die Like a Devil)." They are the unchallenged kings of what is known as black metal. Band members name themselves after demons, including one who calls himself Abaddon. Another member of the group, Manta, says, "We totally believe in the music we play and the subject we sing about. Attending a Venom show is like watching an auto wreck—or better yet, being in one."[25]

Mike Jones, director of promotions for their label, Combat Records, says, "The name of the game is the kids need to rebel. They need their own identity. Your average fifteen-year-old isn't going to sacrifice a goat just because he listened to the Venom album *Hell Awaits*."[26] Combat Records also markets the album of a group called Hades.

The band Celtic Frost released the album, *Emperor's Return*, showing Lucifer with a serpent's tail and twin horns, his snakelike body entwined with three nearly nude women. One member of the band sports a leather bicep armband with an inverted cross. The group Tyrant released an album entitled *Legions of the Dead*, described in advertisements as "a bloodcurdling metallic storm." A European band, Destruction, put out an album called *Infernal Overkill*. The heavy metal label Megaforce Records recently released an album entitled *Blessed Death*, featuring two clerical hands posed prayerfully and rising from hellish flames. *Gates to Purgatory* is the name of an album by the group Running Wild, whose songs include "Soldiers of Hell" and "Diabolic Force."

Before he became a single rock act, singer King Diamond performed with the band Mercyful Fate. It was widely rumored that Diamond anointed his audiences with human blood, filled a doll with pig's entrails, and sacrificed it. On the front of their album, *Metal Forces*, King Diamond is shown clutching a nun's bosom and biting her neck with two streams of blood trickling down her chest. His lyrics declare, "I deny Christ, the deceiver." Diamond says, "I believe in the philosophy of Anton Lavey [head of the Church of Satan]. I don't believe there is a heaven with pearly gates and all those people running around playing harps. The thing I call Satan is the power of the universe that keeps things in balance. Evil is necessary in the world, or how else could you appreciate good?"[27]

The band Grim Reaper featured an album jacket picturing death as a hooded skeleton riding a horse. Skulls dangle from the saddle. The horse's harness has a goat's head and various occult signs, including the pentagram. The back of the album jacket features a circle of black magic hieroglyphics. The group claims the graphics on the album were not their idea. The lyrics were. One tune entitled "See You in Hell" says, "I'll make you an offer you can't refuse." The singer goes on to tell listeners he will take them to the depths of their soul and make them burn when he finally consigns them to hell. An advertisement for the album declared, "The album you'll sell your soul for." Nick Bowcott of the group claims the band is not a black metal band nor involved in the satanic. He declares, "The occult is fun to write about because there's so many interesting directions you can take with your music. Just because you sing about hell doesn't mean you are the devil's disciple."[28] One wonders if such overt satanism can be shrugged off so easily. If the members of Grim Reaper are not the devil's disciples, why do they record whole albums with such lyrics?

Not all occult and satanic influence in music is so obvious, of course. The song "Undercover Angel" illustrates the subtlety by which occult themes sneak into rock music. The singer spoke of a "midnight fantasy" to whom he made love in bed. The song seemed to reflect upon a young man's longings as he dreamed nightly of an imaginary lover, but, in fact, the song was based on the occult phenomenon of the succubus, a human male cohabiting with a materialized female demon spirit. Such songs probably do less harm than the outright satanism of some of the performers mentioned above, but "Undercover Angel" is a good example of a seemingly innocuous song that is, underneath, a flirtation with the world of darkness.

Suppose you discover your child listens to satanic music. Perhaps he owns such records. As a concerned parent, you want to take action. You want your house to serve the Lord, a desire that will be profoundly threatened if your child is exposed to such music. What can you do?

Pose the following questions to him:

Question #1—Does purchasing a record enhance the artist's popularity and more widely disperse his philosophy?

When a rock artist is idolized by millions of impressionable youth, his outlook on the demonic may be more inviting because of his commercial success. Certainly, no Christian young person would want his peers to experiment with the occult simply because his favorite rock star recommends it.

Question #2—If music has the ability to convey spiritual power as well as melodic and rhythmic content, what is implied when a musician admits contact with the powers of darkness?

In the biblical case of King David, we see that music can facilitate the presence of the Holy Spirit and hinder the work of evil spirits. Pagan rituals conjure demons by rhythmic repetition and idolatrous devotion. Beware, then, of musical performers who misuse creativity to invest occult power in their art.

Question #3—Is it possible to listen to the music of a rock artist involved in the occult and appreciate his talent without being affected by his lyrics or demonic inspiration?

Just as the anointing of the Holy Spirit rests upon soul-lifting music, Satan can convey a counterfeit unction to create an unhealthy spiritual atmosphere. Whether the person listening to an occult rock song consciously hears the words is irrelevant. The subconscious mind, the seat of the soul, is affected.

Question #4—When the record album of an artist involved in the occult is purchased, what are the implications of Christ's words in Matthew 12:30: "He that is not with me is against me"?

All occult phenomena come from Satan, the enemy of God. Therefore, anyone who advocates demonic practices declares himself in opposition to the Lord. The Devil relentlessly pursues your child's sympathy, so pray that he makes the right decision.

NOTES

1. *People*, June 23, 1980.   2. *Billboard*, July 7, 1980, p. 7.   3. *Rolling Stone*, June 25, 1981, p. 49.   4. *Billboard*, December 10, 1977, p. 38.   5. *Circus*, November 1974, p. 64.   6. *Crawdaddy*, February 1978, p. 18.   7. *Circus*, January 19, 1977, p. 23.   8. *Rolling Stone*, January 26, 1978, p. 14.   9. *Circus*, August 16, 1976, p. 30.   10. *Circus*, June 22, 1978, p. 15.   11. *Circus*, April 30, 1981, pp. 45-46.   12. *Circus*, October 12, 1976, p. 41.   13. *Rolling Stone*, October 26, 1972, p. 12.   14. *Rolling Stone*, December 16, 1976, p. 11.   15. *Time*, December 16, 1974, p. 39.   16. *Newsweek*, May 10, 1976, p. 121.   17. *People*, July 19, 1976, p. 51.   18. *Circus*, October 13, 1977, p. 28.   19. *Circus*, May 26, 1977, p. 52.   20. *Rolling Stone*, December 16, 1976, p. 61.   21. *Billboard*, October 12, 1974, p. 38.   22. *Circus*, December 22, 1977, p. 12.   23. *Hit Parader*, July 1975, p. 16.   24. *New Times*, Vol. 16, No. 22, p. 9.   25. *Hit Parader*, November 1985, p. 20.   26. *USA Today*, August 18, 1986, p. 2D.   27. *Grabbith*, Vol. 1, No. 5.   28. *Hit Parader*, December 1985, p. 59.

EIGHT
HEAVY METAL MADNESS

Heavy metal isn't a new element on a physics periodic chart, nor is it an industrial product conceived for the construction industry. Heavy metal is a kind of rock music spawned in the late sixties, considered dead during the seventies, but alive and well in the eighties.

Among the most popular heavy metal bands are AC/DC, Iron Maiden, Dio, Scorpions, Judas Priest, Ratt, Ozzy Osbourne, Motley Crue, Quiet Riot, Deep Purple, Twisted Sister, Armored Saint, Metallica, Dokken, Grim Reaper, Queensryche, Keel, WASP, Raven, Black Sabbath, Van Halen, Aerosmith, Accept, Loudness, Krokus, Blue Oyster Cult, Def Leppard, and Triumph.

Those who listen to heavy metal are called "head bangers," alluding to the musical energy and excitement that makes fans bang their heads on the foot of the concert stage. The term *heavy metal* supposedly came from a description of its sound, comparing the crashing, clashing guitar chords to a raucous Detroit assembly line stamping automobile parts from sheets of steel.

Rock critic Lester Bangs defines it specifically: "A heavily distorted, highly amplified form of pop music that evolved from the blues/rock music of the late sixties. In its classic form, it features plodding, unsubtle rhythms, screaming vocals, primal wailing guitar sounds, and macho-posturing lyrics dealing with sex, drugs, and rock 'n' roll."

A more analytical description was featured in *Rolling Stone* magazine, which declared, "Heavy metal is boy's music using electric guitars as a desperate and obvious symbol of adolescent, hormonal hysteria. Heavy metal may not be high art, but it is heroic and its heroes assume one of several poses: sexual athletes (AC/DC); the ascendency to manhood via a variant on knife-wielding juvenile delinquency (Twisted Sister); insane instrumental virtuosity (Yngwie Malmsteen); the good old transcendent rock 'n' roll party ethic (Scorpions and Ratt); or any combination thereof (Motley Crue)."[1]

Make no mistake about it, heavy metal is popular. *Billboard,* the music industry's trade publication, commented, "Heavy metal has proved immune to shifting musical/cultural trends. Since 1980, no other pop music form has accounted for greater record sales. Of the top-grossing live acts in 1985, 20.6 percent were metal artists, while for 1985's last quarter nearly one of every three top-grossing acts featured hard rockers."[2] MTV popularized heavy metal by visually bringing into the living room leather, whips, chains, and women in tortured submission, with an excess of blood and gore.

Heavy metal is more than music. It's an image conjured by the artist's actions and stage antics. Heavy metal fashion features leather costumes adorned with spikes, studs, and chains. Rock magazines catering to the heavy metal trade advertise barbaric necklaces and wristbands with sharpened barbs.

Heavy metal's philosophy can be summed up in the words of Twisted Sister's lead singer, Dee Snyder: "The essential element of heavy metal is the same as it was in the original 1950s rock 'n' roll. Parents hate it."

Ronnie James Dio says, "Good heavy metal is so rough and tumble it pushes you right to the edge of madness."

The leader of the band Motor Head describes his craft by saying, "If our band moved next door to you, your lawn would die."[3]

One metal band leader offers a simpler definition: "Music to kill your parents by."

With its power chord catechism, heavy metal features guitar-based music played by long-haired sneering men adorned in leather. Describing its resurging popularity in the 1980s, one rock periodical said, "Just when the world was supposed to be safe for New Wave music, what should rear its leather-clad, lipstick-smeared image but heavy metal, rising up from the smoking remains of a million shredded speaker cones, nastier, noisier, and more popular than ever."[4]

Heavy metal has its sinister side. A group called Sodom released an album entitled *Obsessed by Cruelty*, its record jacket portraying a skeletal death figure with clawlike fingers dripping blood. The group Destruction released an album entitled *Eternal Devastation*. Another band called Cirith Ungol entitled its album *One Foot in Hell*. The debut album of Diamond Rexx was called *Hand of the Damned*. The group Heretic entitled one of their albums *Torture Knows No Boundaries*. Combat Records produced the album *Darkness Descends* by a band called Dark Angel. Combat has another band called Possessed, whose album *Beyond the Gates* stylizes the *s* in the word *Gates* by extending the bottom of the *s* into a forked tail.

The group Metal Church displayed on the front of one album jacket a house with an open door, through which two eyes peered from darkness. Their song "Ton of Bricks" described someone ripping and kicking until "blood begins to flow." Other lyrics suggest, "I live to eat your bones."

An album by Megadeth was named *Peace Sells . . . But Who's Buying?* The cover pictured New York City in shambles and the United Nations lying in ruins, as jet bombers fly overhead. One song entitled "The Conjuring" described a satanic ceremony. The singer said, "I am the devil's advocate," inviting the listener to "join me in my infernal depths," which he defined as "Mephisto's hall of fame." He concluded by saying, "I've got your soul."

Minor metal groups competed for popularity. An album by the band Bitch showed a scantily clad, leather-laden harlot holding a whip in one hand and a chain in the other. The group Savage Grace released an album picturing a woman with her face bruised, blood streaming from a corner of her mouth. She stands in front of a chopping block looking fearfully at a hooded executioner holding an axe.

One rock periodical called the group Slayer the "kings of black metal."[5] A member of the band was pictured wearing a pentagram medallion and two inverted crosses. The Los Angeles group records for Columbia, who decided not to release their album *Reign in Blood* because of its sadistic lyrics and Nazi references. A fan declared of Slayer, "They are the real thing. They are almost scary but in a good sort of way."[6] Vocalist and bass player Tom Araya says, "We enjoy the type of music we do because it's really interesting stuff to write about. Who needs another love song? We like to explore the dark side of things."[7] When asked about the group's satanic image, Araya answered, "We have a black image, but it doesn't necessarily mean we're satanic. It's a free country. The idea behind Slayer is energy, power, and aggression." When a reporter probed further as to whether he worshiped the devil, Araya responded, "I plead the Fifth on that. I have my own beliefs, and if my beliefs fall in that direction, then maybe I am."[8]

The band Metallica toured with Ozzy Osbourne. One critic said of their performances, "In this world of blow-dried heavy metal heroes, Metallica is not the prettiest of sights. When God gave out the tight satin pants and peroxide, Metallica wasn't standing in the right line."[9] Their song "Leper Messiah" is about American television religion. When asked by a reporter if they were into the typical "rape and pillage" of heavy metal, Lars Ulrich of the band, said, "I think everyone in the band contributes to that department."[10] Though their albums are laced with four-letter words, they have recorded tunes like "Master of Puppets," an antidrug anthem.

The band Raven includes a member named Wacko who wears a football helmet and pounds the drums with his head, fists, and forearms. John Gallagher, bass player of the group, says of Wacko, "He's a lunatic. If he hadn't been a rock 'n' roller he'd be in a mental hospital."[11] Their album *Stay Hard* shows a naked muscle man's bare chest from the neck to just above the pubic hairline and a woman's hand ripping the skin off his chest. Underneath is the name of the group and the album title. On the back, Wacko is pictured in his helmet. One member of the group is holding a police truncheon in his hand. The group admits they are somewhat violent, even when they record. During a recent session, Wacko destroyed his drum kit, and two other members of the band broke four instruments each. Gallagher says, "As far as the injuries go, we just treat them as being in a rock 'n' roll band. Playing on stage is like playing a football game to us—it's very physical. If it means getting a few burns from the pyro when it goes off, or having scars from instruments crashing into us, that's the way it is."[12]

A label called Metal Blade Records, whose symbol is an axe blade dripping with blood, has released an album called *Metal Massacre Seven* with the symbol of death shown holding a scythe in one hand and a leashed Doberman pinscher in the other. An album by Hyrax is called *Raging Violence*. The jacket shows a head full of bullet holes, the skull splintering and the face grimacing in pain. The group Predator has an album entitled *Easy Prey*. A man standing under a pier on a beach gawks at a woman walking by in a bikini.

He reaches around the pole as if to attack her. The group Blood Lust produced an album entitled *Guilty as Sin*. The group Thrust entitled their album *Fist Held High*, the jacket adorned with a spiked ball.

One group calls itself Satan. The cover of its album, *Court in the Act*, shows a robed skeletal figure rising out of a misty cloud. A bony hand points to the name Satan. More absurd is the heavy metal band, The Mentors, whose album is called *You Axed for It*. A review of the album said, "If it isn't a joke, then it is the sickest LP in many years. The musicians have names like Sickie Wifebeater, and they play incredibly tuneless numbers like 'Clap Queen' and 'Sandwich of Love.' Incidentally, it's on Death Records."[13]

The band Anthrax named itself after a deadly infectious disease. Guitarist Scott Ian says, "Our goal is to be the most deadly metal band on the face of the earth. If you don't like your music loud and fast and furious, you'd better not bother with us."[14] Onstage, they dress in a sinister array of biker gear. Ian says, "We're a little sick. We don't like things that are safe and pretty. We are off-the-wall. We're there to assault you. We don't want to take any prisoners. We either want you to be on our side, or we'll blow you away."[15]

Rockie Shayes of the group Wrathchild wears the usual heavy metal regalia of leather and studs and has dozens of sharp three-inch spikes sticking out of his costume. Their stage show features naked women, whips, and chains. Their debut album was entitled *Stakk Attackk*. Vocalist Shayes says, "I admit we're loud, lewd, and a little more than crazy, but what's wrong with it? If our wicked minds can think of something depraved, there's no doubt we'll put it to music and record it. We want our music to be loud and obnoxious."[16]

The group Lizzy Borden features a macabre stage show. Their theatrical bloodletting is based on the band's namesake, the nineteenth-century murderer, Lizzy Borden, who killed her parents with an ax. Lizzy Borden's songs include "Love Kills" and "Terror on the Town." They've been banned from playing in certain areas, and their theatrics have caused some major bands to shy away from using them as an opening act. The lead vocalist for the group says, "Although we like beheadings and killings—that's the stuff we grew up on watching TV—we're a product of our environment. We're an American rock 'n' roll band, and the new album just showed the things we loved—like sex and violence."[17]

The group Quiet Riot is more sexual than sinister. Rudy Sarzo of the group says, "The reason I got into music was because of the girls. I'm still sexually depraved."[18] Their hit song "Cum on Feel the Noiz" invites ladies in the audience to "rock your boys" (the verb *rock* is substituted with a sexual expletive in live concerts). Kevin DeBrow of the group once addressed a Big Apple audience by saying, "I hear people in New York are real nasty and that you like to do nasty things in the backseat of cars. As I see it, you need three things for a good party. First, you need the right kind of medicine. Secondly, you need the proper kind of consumable substances and, third, you need noisemakers."[19]

Parents who are reading this may find it all hard to believe. Indeed, if it weren't all so perverse, it might be funny. A 1985 film, *This Is Spinal Tap,* had adults laughing hysterically at the music and life-styles of a fake British heavy metal band, Spinal Tap. The film was a spoof, a mock documentary that let audiences roar at the antics of the oh-so-serious heavy metal performers. But, strangely enough, many youth attended the film and believed they were watching a real group on tour. (Some critics, not realizing the whole film was a satire, criticized the filmmakers for making a documentary about a group no one had heard of before!) The absurd (and obscene) lyrics and stage antics of the nonexistent group made adults laugh, but many did not realize that the spoof was no exaggeration of heavy metal. What seemed like an amusing yarn about overgrown adolescents singing lewd songs was taken seriously by young viewers. And the effect of such music isn't funny at all.

Heavy metal audiences are young. A survey of those attending heavy metal concerts showed that 56 percent of the crowd was seventeen years of age or younger. Two-thirds were male. Only 9 percent of the heavy metal audience was twenty-four or older.[20] Such facts disturb California psychologist, Dr. Richard Sherman. He says, "Some of these groups project an image that can trigger violence, even blood and devil worship. When children choose them as role models, they're learning to go against the basic values of society."[21]

More sexy than satanic, the Philadelphia-based band Cinderella is an example of rock 'n' roll sexism at its worst. Their tune "Shake Me" describes a one-night stand with repeated acts of intercourse. The song speaks of the female sex partner still going strong in the morning. In "Nothing for Nothing," Cinderella went beyond sensuality into despair. The song speaks of the end of life approaching, with a hole of doubt getting deeper. In the end, according to the song, life amounts to "nothin' for nothin'."

Rebellion and satanism combine explosively during heavy metal concerts. Thousands of teenagers flash the so-called "evil hand" or satanic salute. Entrepreneurs have marketed a giant three-foot-tall "evil hand." Ads proclaim the synthetic satanic salutes can be "seen across a coliseum floor."

Heavy metal band leader Blackie Lawless of the group WASP says of such concerts, "To me, rock is theater, electric vaudeville. It's a place where you can do about anything and get away with it. It's a zone where rules and restrictions are just totally thrown out the window. It's like controlled anarchy. We spit blood and throw raw pieces of meat into the audience. We're not trying to make a great social statement. We're just trying to entertain."[22]

A controversy has brewed as to whether cities have the right to ban heavy metal groups. Rock ordinances have kept some bands out of certain cities. During a recent Seattle concert by Judas Priest, a young man was stabbed to death. Whether the atmosphere created by Judas Priest contributed to his death is debatable.

An organization called Back in Control Center urges parents to "de-metal" kids who go off the deep end. The center says parents should take away heavy metal records, paraphernalia, and monitor clothes and friendships. Darlene Pettinicchio calls herself the center's "heavy metal consultant." She says, "We're talking about kids who become totally absorbed in punk or heavy metal, who dress like their favorite band, who act like band members, who get their philosophies and beliefs from band members."[23]

Pettinicchio is rightfully disturbed. As the member of one heavy metal band put it, "Satan is an outcast. I'd rather be an outcast than conform to the majority. We want to be outcasts. We want to be different."[24]

Why do kids go to heavy metal concerts? Jim Koziowiski of Combat Records says, "It's almost tribal in a sense. Everybody jammed in together. They get sweaty and slam dance into each other. It's like rams mating in the mountains. Everyone in the audience is like you. You run up on the stage and dive off as far as you can—it's called stage diving—because you know they'll catch you. It's a sense of brotherhood like Woodstock."[25]

In contrast to the death message found in heavy metal music, Jesus promises in Scripture, "I will give unto him that is athirst of the fountain of the water of life freely" (Revelation 21:6). Heavy metal bands sing about forbidden behavior, immorality, and rebellion, and its fascination with hell and death is prevalent. But it overlooks the fact that one day death itself will be cast into the eternal flames of the lake of fire.

Though hell has been prepared for death, demons, and the devil, Revelation 20:15 also warns us it is the eternal destination for "whosoever was not found written in the Book of Life." Death fills the themes of much heavy metal music, but Jeremiah 21:8 says, "Thus sayeth the Lord, behold I set before you the way of life and death." The way of life is through Christ. You can lead your child to choose him instead of the madness of heavy metal.

NOTES

1. *Rolling Stone,* (no date).   2. *Billboard,* Heavy Metal Issue, 1985, p. 81.
3. *Dallas Morning News,* November 25, 1984.   4. *Rolling Stone,* September 27, 1984, p. 83.   5. *Hit Parader,* September 1986, p. 48.   6. *Hit Parader,* September 1986, p. 48.   7. Ibid., p. 48.   8. *Hit Parader,* May 1987, p. 65.   9. *Circus,* July 31, 1986.   10. *Hit Parader,* August 1986, p. 17.   11. *Hit Parader,* June 1986, p. 19.   12. *Hit Parader,* September 1986, p. 38.   13. *Hit Parader,* July 1986, p. 54.   14. *Hit Parader,* June 1986, p. 60.   15. Ibid.   16. *Hit Parader,* May 1985, p. 42.   17. *Hit Parader,* May 1987, p. 34.   18. *Hit Parader,* December 1983, p. 14.   19. *Circus,* December 31, 1983, p. 21.   20. *Billboard,* July 6, 1985, p. 22.   21. *Woman's World,* April 2, 1985, p. 6.   22. *Hit Parader,* October 1985, p. 33.   23. *USA Today,* October 18, 1986, p. 2D.   24. *USA Today,* August 18, 1986, p. 2D.   25. Ibid.

N I N E
I WANT MY MTV!

A video revolution is taking place, a vid-blitz that has shaken Hollywood and the record business, establishing a whole new way of relating to music. What began as brief film clips promoting rock songs has turned into a multimillion-dollar industry.

MTV—Music Television—is a cable TV channel that offers round-the-clock music videos. Launched on August 1, 1981, MTV now boasts 13.5 million viewers, mostly between the ages of twelve and thirty-four.[1] A study of MTV viewers shows that an average viewer spends sixty-eight minutes a day watching MTV (ninety minutes on Saturdays and Sundays).[2] Sixty-three percent of the audience is under age twenty-five.[3] The median age of MTV viewers is twenty-three, the median income is $30,000, and more than half of those over age eighteen are college-educated.[4] MTV income in 1984 was $71 million, and in 1986 it had ballooned to $97 million.[5] Considered a risky oddity when it was launched, the twenty-four-hour music video channel has become a fixture in American life.

Robert Pittman, a former radio program director, was the original executive officer of MTV, a name he invented. Of his audience, Pittman says, "These are people who grow up with television, who learn to do their homework, listen to the radio, and watch television all at the same time. For these people we needed to create a form that was nonlinear, using mood and emotion to create an atmosphere."[6]

Blatantly aiming MTV at the adolescent mind, Pittman says, "Kids around eighteen use music to define their identity the way people in middle age use cars and homes."[7]

Music videos create a strange fantasy world where the bizarre is normal and few coherent story lines exist. The videos are mostly blatant visual gluttony, often saturated with sex, violence, and quick camera cuts that bombard the senses. Videos combine the power of rock music with thirty years of television technology and the razzle-dazzle of short, high-budget commercials. The result is programming that is short, slick, and punchy. This is television that is seductive and addictive, especially to pre-teens. And for the first time in history, the raunchiness that many rock groups present in their concerts is now available in American living rooms—twenty-four hours a day.

Rock videos don't aim for the intellect. Jeff Stein, who directed the Cars' video "You Might Think," says, "All my stuff is for audiences raised on television, drugs, and rock 'n' roll. It's easy to come up with video scripts if you just take a lot of hallucinogens in your younger days."[8]

There are three basic kinds of videos: narratives, like Thomas Dolby's "She Blinded Me with Science," that tell a loosely connected story; videos that string together images providing no plot line, such as David Bowie's "Let's Dance," and concert videos, like Squeeze's "Tempted," with the band lip-synching lyrics while the camera rolls.[9]

The images are often repulsive. In one video a nude woman in chains appears in the background while a man in the foreground sharpens a razor. In another, wild-haired, scantily clad vixens crawl on the outside of a steel cage, craving the bodies inside. Enslaved women appear in bondage with scenes of nudity and fondling. Most teens would recognize these scenes from videos of Billy Idol's "Dancing with Myself," the Scorpions' "Rock You Like a Hurricane," and Van Halen's "Oh, Pretty Woman."[10]

In a Twisted Sister video, a father who objects to his son's music is blown out of the window when the errant offspring plays his guitar. A Ratt video shows a polite gathering in a posh home, which is interrupted when the rock band playing upstairs falls through the ceiling, lands on the dinner table, and scatters food and guests.

The now defunct gay group Frankie Goes to Hollywood produced

"Two Tribes," a video depicting two actors portraying Ronald Reagan and the late Soviet leader Chernenko. The two battle in a ring, and the Chernenko character grabs Reagan by the genitals.

A video entitled "This Is Mine" by the group Heaven 17 features a relatively clean-cut band hanging around on the streets. They rob a bank, and the members are lifted in a helicopter as they throw money into the air. The message seems to be that of many videos: Authority and rules are to be flouted whenever possible.

The Georgia Satellite's video "Keep Your Hands to Yourself" shows a supposedly chaste young woman fending off advances. In the end, however, she gives in. The video's final shot shows her in a white wedding gown, obviously pregnant. The Poison video "Talk Dirty to Me" is introduced with a sultry female voice declaring, "I can't wait to get my hands all over you." The lead singer states that he's going to take her down to the basement and lock the door so she can talk dirty to him.

Sexy singer David Lee Roth, formerly with the group Van Halen, carried his sensuous stage act into living rooms with his "Yankee Rose" video. Simulating copulation, Roth gave viewers three minutes of overt sensuality that had no parallel in previous videos. The camera apparently had a fixation on the crotches and behinds of Roth and his band.

"That Ain't Love" by REO Speedwagon simulates a camp revival meeting in the 1930s style. The preacher at the pulpit is REO Speedwagon's lead singer, bellowing out a rock tune. Suggestively clad women come forward at the end of the "sermon," not to repent but to dance with abandon. In Triumph's "Just One Night" video, a miniskirted maiden saunters sensuously down the street while the singer pleads, "Take me, I'm yours—just one night." Typical of the quickly changing imagery of rock videos, the video for Cutting Crew's "I Just Died in Your Arms" intersperses images of fruit, the band's lead singer, and parts of a woman's anatomy.

One of the most offensive videos is Whitesnake's "Still of the Night." In it, a sexily dressed girl is seen ascending and descending stairs, pulling up her skirt to maximize the exposure of her legs. As she poses suggestively, the video cuts directly to scenes of band members doing pelvic thrusts. At one point the girl lies screaming and blindfolded on a couch. The lead singer sings, "I just want to get close to you, feel your body heat." At the end, a figure in a long

black coat (the girl? the lead singer?) is manhandled by two police-
men and thrown in the back of a van. When the doors close, we see
the word SEX in large letters, written in blood.

Even some of the tamer videos seems to have a sexual obsession.
Steve Winwood sang about a "Higher Love," but the video for the
song indicated that the cameramen had a fixation on women's
breasts.

Though MTV claims to censor nudity and violence, rock videos
show as much as possible. David Bowie's "China Girl" video had
beach scenes with bare bottoms. Duran Duran's "Hungry Like a
Wolf" video has a wrestling match with a sinister, semi-nude native
woman. Laura Branigan's "Self-control" video was too hot for
record company executives. They snipped out segments showing
Laura at a sex club with a masked lover passionately kissing parts of
her body. The video for the J. Geils Band's "Centerfold" had shots
of half-naked women.

Will MTV censor anything? Robert Pittman has reportedly said
he would show anything as long as it wasn't "naked women running
around throwing babies out of trucks."[11]

With that rough guideline, almost anything goes. Madonna's
video for "Like a Virgin" shows her writhing on a bed in a wedding
gown, dancing half-clothed on a gondola, and wearing a white
underwire corset. US magazine said the video was "a sum of her
body parts stretching old-fashioned titillation to new limits." The
queen of wanton ways, Madonna writhes in sexual frustration for
the video "Burning Up." At one point she sits down in the middle of
the road, asking, "Do you want to see me down on my knees?" In
the extremely offensive video for "Open Your Heart to Me," she is
working in a peep show and, at the video's end, scampering off
down the road with a young boy, suggesting that she is going to
initiate him sexually. Madonna's message to girls seems to be that
their main role in life is to be a "boy toy."

This is typical of rock videos. Women are pictured as nym-
phomaniacs wearing spiked heels and black lingerie, parading
through the rock 'n' roll jungle anticipating seduction. Sadomasochism often enters into the sexual experience, promoting rapist
fantasies that lurk in the recesses of the American male's mind. In
videos, women are often the eager victims of sexual conquest,
offering their services to rock star studs demanding a sexual fix.

Such blatant sexism worries Dr. Victor Strasburger, Director of

Adolescent Medicine for the American Academy of Pediatrics Task Force on Television. Dr. Strasburger says, "Listening to 'Let's Spend the Night Together' didn't get any girl to hop into bed with me or anyone else. But seeing a sexy video can teach you that if you're not sexually active, there's something wrong with you. Once you've depicted the song, you've magnified the effect a hundred-fold."[12]

Sex isn't the only thing that needs censoring. Violence has been part of rock videos since the beginning. David Horowitz, president of MTV, declares, "I don't think there's an excessive amount of violence. . . . We will not run videos that include senseless violence, explicit sexual activity, nudity, profanity, or drug abuse."[13] But the National Coalition on Television Violence (NCTV) studied nine hundred rock videos and reported that 46 percent contained violence or indicated violence. Of the nine hundred, 13 percent had sadistic violence with an attacker deriving pleasure from his violent act. The NCTV found an average of 17.9 violent acts per hour, with 22 percent of all videos containing violence against men and women.[14] The coalition also discovered that violent lyrics in rock music have increased 115 percent since 1963, and sadistic violence appears more frequently on MTV than any other channel.[15]

Other research supports these findings. A professor of journalism at the University of Georgia reviewed three hundred videos and found that 56 percent contained violence, and two-thirds of that was linked with sex.[16] The director of a Canadian coalition against violent entertainment says a survey of videos done by his group revealed that 35 percent of the videos surveyed featured sexual violence.[17]

With young children watching these scenes of women in chains and people being tortured and shot, psychologist Joyce Brothers is worried. "Teenagers have not fused the idea of love and sex. So when you teach them that violence and sex are related, it's extremely dangerous for their future behavior."[18]

Even people in the rock music industry have expressed concern. One disc jockey says, "The scary element is that kids are at the most impressionable point of their lives, and I would not want any of my sons to get their attitudes about sex and violence or women from music videos."[19]

Children may not understand that licking ice cream cones can suggest oral sex or that leather and chains suggest sadomasochism, but the subliminal impact is there. Marcia Kinder, a professor at the University of Southern California, is concerned about these effects: "Like dreams, rock videos have short scenes and abrupt shifts which encourage the viewer to process them in his or her dream life."[20]

Peggy Charren of Action for Children's Television, a parent group, says, "What I worry about is kids learning that it's fun to beat people up and that sex may mean chains as often as hugs." Les Garland, MTV's vice president of programming, responds, "You can lodge these same allegations against every other channel."[21] This isn't much consolation to parents.

Dr. Eli Newburger, Director of the Family Development Studies at Children's Hospital in Boston says, "Children are being bombarded with messages of violence and sexuality that are very confusing and suggest easy ways out of complex situations."[22]

In Canada, the Ontario Teacher's Federation is so concerned it has released a teacher's resource book designed to warn students about the influence of music videos. According to the book, "While the potential for this art form remains great, most videos consistently blur the distinction between reality and fantasy."

Teachers and parents do well to be concerned, for there is no doubt that youth and children spend a great deal of time watching videos. Halloween parties have not been the same since the advent of MTV; children attend them dressed as Madonna, Cyndi Lauper, and other popular video artists. Teachers report that grade schoolers dress like the performers in rock videos. One educator declared, "A kid came to school wearing studded neck and wrist bands. He didn't even know how to read, but he picked up symbols of the culture."[23] This isn't the only effect; some parents report that their children are unable to sleep after watching nightmarish videos.[24] What seems as innocuous as an old-time horror movie to adults may be terrifying to a young child.

Oddly enough, rock videos are now used as educational tools with children. Dr. Michael Bell, a former teacher, is a language expert who has experimented with teaching children with reading problems. Dr. Bell produced "color sounds," a special program designed to enhance grammatical skills and reading comprehension. He shows children videos of rock singers like David Bowie. While the video plays, the words appear on the screen, and certain words light up in different colors to distinguish between parts of speech.[25]

It's certainly a sign of the times that children are being taught grammar and linguistics by someone like David Bowie. But if videos can perform an educational function, it is far outweighed by the dangers of daily viewings of this questionable art form.

Perhaps the biggest danger of rock videos is the willingness of parents to surrender their children to the tube. Children are used to the flashy images and slick techniques of "Sesame Street," but these same techniques sell sex and violence on MTV. Parents may see rock videos as an innocuous baby-sitter, but the baby-sitter is also a teaching tool, one that teaches things the parents would not approve of.

Dare we hope for improvements in MTV's programming? The Rock Against Drugs Organization aired public service announcements on MTV in a cooperative campaign involving California's attorney general's office and Pepsi. MTV donated $3 million worth of airtime, plus creative contributions. Ads featured such performers as Genesis, Cinderella, the Bangles, Lou Reed, Kiss, and Belinda Carlisle.[26] While this is admirable, the negative impact of most rock videos—and, indeed, of rock music in general—cannot be denied. Anti-drug ads by a handful of performers do not cancel out the sexual and violent nature of so much rock video programming.

No matter how negative the influence of rock videos is, they seem to be here to stay, and their impact has reached beyond MTV. To expand its market, MTV spun off VH-1, a twenty-four-hour channel aimed for adults and featuring soft rock artists. Launched January 1, 1985, VH-1 aimed for the 25-54 age bracket. Though few thought it would survive, and MTV management projected only 5 million subscribers, VH-1 boasted 11.9 million subscribers at the end of the first year. The new channel does not air some of the more offensive (and youth-oriented) videos seen on MTV. On weekends it includes some creative videos called "New Visions," videos accompanying contemporary instrumental music. It also features some artists, like Amy Grant, who could not get airtime on the more sensational MTV. VH-1's vice-president of marketing, Tom Lucas, stated, "Adult contemporary is the most popular format in the radio industry."[27] Regrettably, the softer, more artistic approach of the videos on VH-1 is not typical of the youth-directed material on MTV. Though some videos air on both channels, MTV still seems to prefer the sex-and-violence formula.

While MTV and VH-1 are the only round-the-clock video channels, many of the networks and local channels have programs with
rock videos. Pounding rock scores are now the background for
many regular TV series. The idea for the series "Miami Vice" was
jotted on a piece of paper at NBC programming headquarters. The
note read, "MTV cops." Lee Katzin, a director for "Miami Vice,"
said bluntly, "The show was written for an MTV audience."[28]
Cable channel HBO (Home Box Office) joined the video trend by
featuring concert specials to attract youth.

The success of videos has spawned special video awards. Gram-
mys, considered the top awards in the music industry, are now
awarded not only for sound recordings but for videos as well. There
is also a special awards ceremony for videos alone.

Music and movies have gone together ever since sound was a part
of film, but this is more true now than ever before. Rock videos
promote the films in which the songs appear, and vice versa. Some
contemporary movie directors learned their craft by directing
videos. The 1984 film *Electric Dreams* was one of the first major
films directed by a video director, and his training was obvious in
the film's thin story line, in its quickly changing visuals, and
especially in its use of music to sustain audiences' interest.

Videos are not just a part of TV programming and movies.
Record stores now sell full-length videocassettes. Buyers can
purchase their favorite artist's album, or opt for the video version of
the album. With stereo available now on VCRs and on videocassettes, none of the sound quality is lost in the video versions. Record
companies now have video divisions for producing and marketing
these products. And many of the album-length videos are even more
sexual and violent than the already offensive videos seen on TV.

The economic impact of music videos is enormous. A survey by
Nielsen indicated that of the nine album purchases the average MTV
viewer makes in one year, four are influenced by videos. And in a
time when gruelling concert tours are becoming a less than profit-
able means of exposure for a new group, rock videos are an excellent
means for breaking in new and foreign (particularly British) acts in
the U.S. The opportunity to present both sound and visual presence
to a wide audience has resulted in improved radio play and record
distribution for many new acts. (Regrettably, the wide exposure of
visual presence has led to the success of some artists of questionable

talent—Madonna, for example—who probably would not have succeeded on their musical abilities alone.)

Not all artists are caught up in the video craze. Van Halen's album *5150* hit Number One on the charts with no help from video exposure. The group Journey released their popular album *Raised on Radio* with no video clips. The manager of Journey stated, "Why should we go out and put ourselves at the mercy of the video director to conceptualize our music and to put a very short-lived, limited lifespan visual accompaniment?"[29] His words must have carried weight, since the budget for *Raised on Radio* included $300,000 for video production. But this is exceptional, since most artists have jumped on the video bandwagon, recognizing the exposure that videos offer.

Rock videos are so popular that their producers are awarded equal billing with Hollywood entrepreneurs. Their names are as familiar in the record industry as Steven Spielberg's is to moviegoers. Top video producers have been known to spend over a quarter of a million for three minutes of sights and sounds.[30] Michael Jackson's notorious "Thriller" video cost over a million dollars to produce.

In spite of the impact of videos, the future of MTV is unknown. In April 1986, Nielsen showed that ratings were down. To combat the loss of viewers, MTV diversified its all-video approach by adding reruns of "The Monkees," live coverage of spring break in Daytona, Florida, and wrestling awards. Half-hour sitcoms were being considered, and the parent company had suggested adding a weekly movie to the schedule. Determined to counter the ratings drop, the new MTV president, Tom Freston, brought out heavy metal videos in full force and relegated Top Forty ballads to the tamer VH-1. MTV became the youth channel, the place where the programming was strictly for youth, not the people who like Paul McCartney, Linda Ronstadt, and Julio Iglesias.

Freston, who took over from MTV founder Robert Pittman in January 1986, replaced the MTV VJs (video jocks, the MTV hosts) with younger personalities, such as Frank Zappa's son, Dweezil. A daily half-hour afternoon slot was devoted solely to heavy metal. Like rock music at its core, MTV is now the "rebel" channel, the channel that says, in effect, "No parents or other authorities allowed here."

In all fairness to the artists and the producers of videos, many rock videos show genuine creativity. As in most art forms, there are people in the video business who do not feel the need to resort to sex and violence in order to create interesting works. A-ha's "Take on Me," Men at Work's "Who Can It Be Now?" Queen's "A Kind of Magic," Phil Collins's "Land of Confusion," Kate Bush's "Cloud-busting," and Madness's "Our House" are some videos that show that performers can do more than generate bizarre, unsettling images. Many Christian rock artists—Amy Grant, DeGarmo and Key, and many others—now produce quality videos. These are a welcome alternative to many of the secular products.

Unfortunately, the videos that show some intelligence and creativity are interspersed with the more dominant sex-and-violence formula videos. These are, as the words of the parent groups and psychologists quoted earlier indicate, producing harmful effects, effects that may be difficult to measure. It may take years of exposure to hundreds of videos before youth are measurably affected. Incessant stereotyping of sex and the glamorization of violence must have an insidious cumulative effect on viewers, especially when the immoral behavior is portrayed as stylish and acceptable. No single rock video is going to destroy America's moral fiber, but the genre as a whole is to be indicted for conveying an immoral, anti-Christian view of human beings.

Christian parents should do the obvious thing with MTV—turn it off. It is odd that parents often complain about television's effects on youth but seldom eliminate it. Perhaps a less drastic alternative to doing without television would be to learn to watch it with a critical eye and to discuss it with youth. In the words of Newsweek, "parental supervision may be the sanest answer to any threat posed by music video."[31] Parents can take the time to sit and watch it with youth and then discuss the images. Better, they can find recreation that is more interesting than passively watching the tube. Most sensitive parents would agree with Peggy Charren of Action for Children's Television, who said, "If there are enough alternatives in a child's life, you don't have to worry about what they see on TV."[32]

The worst thing that can happen is that parents abandon their children to the electric baby-sitter that has more interest in profits than in morals. Newsweek called rock videos "something that seems to distil all the worst elements of television into one potent package."[33] If parents cannot learn to discuss the images and morals in this potent package, then the words of MTV founder Robert Pittman may be all too true: "At MTV we don't shoot for the fourteen-year-olds—we own them."[34]

NOTES

1. Mike Clifford and others, *The Harmony Illustrated Encyclopedia of Rock* (New York: Harmony Books, 1986), p. 250.   2. *Billboard*, July 20, 1985, p. 3.   3. *Time*, December 26, 1983, p. 56.   4. Ibid.   5. *USA Today*, April 29, 1986, p. 2D. 6. *Time*, January 7, 1985, p. 42.   7. *Time*, December 26, 1983, p. 63.   8. *Rock Music Update*, Vol. 1., No. 4.   9. *US*, September 12, 1983, p. 20.   10. *Cleveland Plain Dealer*, April 15, 1984, p. 9D.   11. *Rolling Stone*, December 8, 1983, p. 34.   12. *Newsweek*, December 30, 1985, p. 54.   13. *Billboard*, January 12, 1985, p. 33.   14. *Billboard*, December 22, 1984, p. 34.   15. *Christianity Today*, February 17, 1984, p. 36.   16. *Billboard*, January 12, 1985, p. 32.   17. *Billboard*, January 28, 1984, p. 64.   18. *Cleveland Plain Dealer*, April 15, 1984, p. 1D. 19. *USA Today*, May 14, 1986, p. 1D.   20. Ibid.   21. *Newsweek*, June 25, 1984, p. 48.   22. Ibid.   23. *USA Today*, July 31, 1985, p. 2D.   24. *Newsweek*, December 30, 1985, p. 54. 25. *Dallas Morning News*, March 25, 1984, p. 4.   26. *USA Today*, March 9, 1987, p. 3D.   27. *USA Today*, May 12, 1986, p. 3D.   28. *Billboard*, November 23, 1985.   29. *Billboard*, April 26, 1987, p. 1.   30. *Time*, January 7, 1985, p. 42. 31. *Newsweek*, December 30, 1985, p. 56.   32. *U.S. News and World Report*, October 28, 1985, p. 49.   33. *Newsweek*, December 30, 1985, p. 54. 34. *Contemporary Christian Magazine*, July 1985, p. 14.

T E N
"BUT EVERYBODY DOES IT"

Shocked, aren't you? You knew the rock scene was offensive but
never dreamed it could be this bad. If you as a parent are horrified,
at least your awareness has been heightened. You see as never before
the need for appropriate musical standards to be established in your
home.

But wait! Don't grab that hammer and charge into your children's
rooms to break up all their rock albums. You might destroy some
harmless records, which will only convince them of your lunacy.
Let's suppose you do find an objectionable record in their collection.
You allowed them to be purchased in the first place, so don't
suddenly become self-righteous. Breaking those records may also
destroy all remaining lines of communication. You would only
convince your child that the message of the rock singers is true:
Parents don't understand youth.

You need to comprehend that the records you now see as dangerous to your children's spiritual welfare are symptoms, not the
problem. Destroying the effect leaves the cause intact.

After reading this far, you should be convinced that much of the
rock scene is morally questionable and filled with perversion and
debauchery. You're probably thinking, "How could my children
tolerate such filth saturating their minds day after day?"

Most moms and dads ask that question as if it threatens their
success as parents. Now that you know what today's songs and
singers are really saying, it's appalling to think that after all your

efforts to properly train your children, they still violate those principles.

Parent, take the knife away from your throat! You haven't failed. You only underestimated the power of today's culture to induce conformity. Why does your decent, Sunday-school-bred boy wear an Iron Maiden T-shirt? The simple answer is peer pressure.

It would be an eye-opener to spend a day at your children's school and listen to their friends' discussions. In your generation, kids talked about baseball stars and matinee idols. Today, it's rock songs and singers.

Because most students know the words and melodies of every hit on the charts, imagine how your children would feel if they didn't. It's understood in youth culture: Everybody listens to rock. Your children couldn't communicate with their peers if they were unaware of Duran Duran's latest album, David Lee Roth's most recent paramour, and the much publicized drug bust of their favorite group.

Don't take too lightly the "everybody does it" syndrome. Everybody may not do it, but it's all the same if your children think they do. It's ironic that your children probably want to be nonconformist, yet conform to their culture's nonconformity. That's why your son puts on his tattered blue jeans, dons his metal-studded leather jacket, and leaves for a Quiet Riot concert looking like an exact replica of the other ten thousand kids there. You can see right through the conformity of his nonconformity, but he can't.

In this age of depersonalization, this generation is tired of being treated like a number in a computer. They yearn for identity that stands apart from the norm, and since adults establish the criteria for acceptance, rebelling against middle-class values is one way of saying, "You'll have to notice me because I'm different." Different from each other? No, but different from what their rock stars tell them is a corrupt, conformist older generation.

Coupled with the desire for identity is the craving for acceptance. Admit it. You need it as much as your children do. Where do you get acceptance? From social clubs, business associates, and organized institutions. Most of all, you find acceptance with your marriage partner, the one with whom you share your deepest fears and hopes. None of these options are readily available to teenagers.

In addition, youth face sexual pressures of modern life. Many advertised products convey subtle or overt implications that usage insures attraction from the opposite sex. Male-female relationships provide the ultimate indicator of acceptance. Put yourself in your children's position. If they violate the norm of being tuned in and turned on to the world of rock, what potential partners would look at them? They think such deviation indicates social illiteracy.

This is not to condone a permissive attitude toward the cultural temptations that confront your child. His carnal desires cannot be excused. A Christian teenager shouldn't want to attend an Ozzy Osbourne concert, and Christian parents shouldn't permit it. But the purpose of this chapter is to explain adolescent peer pressure for conformity, not idealistic parental desires.

With all the world arrayed against you and the power of the rock culture poised to devour your Christian values, what can a parent do? Be sympathetic to the problems and pressures of youth. Don't overreact to faddish influences. You can confide in your spouse, but your children are convinced that only Twisted Sister and Ratt really understand what they suffer in the throes of adolescence.

Don't fight the rock culture head-on. I may be able to refute the depraved ideologies of today's rock stars, but I have two things you may lack: my background as an entertainer and extensively re-searched knowledge. I probably am more aware of what goes on in the rock scene than most teenagers, advantages unavailable to you.

Don't worry. God has given you something I don't have. The Lord placed inherent respect in your children for the parents who raised them. They may fight with you, but underneath they know you're doing what you think is best. You don't have to know every song and singer on the charts to point out the obvious spiritual deficiencies in their lives and to question your children's identification with their life-styles.

Suppose your children are caught up in the rock culture. Don't release your frustrations in anger. Should you burn your son's Black Sabbath T-shirt and insist he break all his rock albums? You can, but the cure might be worse than the cause.

A friend woke up one day to find her twelve-year-old daughter had papered an entire bedroom wall with pictures of a well-known rock star. She asked my opinion. I told her I felt such prepuberty fascination with rock idols was unhealthy. Directing her attention to her child's pictures, I pointed out the half-bared chest, tight pants with appropriate bulges, and sexy poses.

"You should see what his concerts are like," I explained. "He suggestively dangles the microphone between his legs and caresses his bottom while he sings. Toward the end, he takes off his trousers. He has on an even tighter pair underneath."

The mother blushed at my explicit description of the motives behind preteen rock performers. But she kept her cool and resisted the temptation to rip every picture from the wall in righteous anger. She decided to surreptitiously take down one picture a day and replace each with more appropriate posters and pictures.

Another way to combat peer pressure is to provide contrasting Christian role models. Direct your children to contemporary Christian musicians who understand society's trends but refuse to emulate secular culture.

Your children's affinity for immoral rock songs and singers is a symptom. Getting them to put those kinds of records aside and develop more discerning musical tastes won't be easy. Nothing would please you more than to have them make a clean break with this kind of music, but peer pressure may be too great for them to accomplish overnight such a drastic change in their values. You can pray for their spiritual enlightenment, and this book will show you how that can be achieved. Whether everybody does it or not, you need not doubt the power of prayer.

E L E V E N
THE BEAT GOES ON

After a long day, you finally have a few moments to relax. The dishes are done, the dog's fed, and you can read the last two chapters in that new book. Your husband is captivated by the football game on TV. This is your time of the day. Nothing to bug you. A few minutes of peace and quiet.

You're three pages into chapter ten when . . . *THUMP! THUMP!* It sounds like the roof is caving in, but you know better. Your daughter's bedroom is directly above, and she's supposed to be doing homework. How can she concentrate? The melody line is indecipherable, not to mention the words that come through as barely audible screams and groans. But the *THUMP! THUMP!* does come through.

You try to ignore the booming beat. Why can't she listen to soft, soothing music, the kind you enjoy? It would prepare her mind better to do algebra equations. This isn't even music, and your patience is exhausted.

"George, do you hear what your daughter is doing? No wonder she gets Cs. That beat is driving her crazy! She'll just have to turn the stereo off."

"Uh-huh," George replies. Obviously, fourth down on the one-yard line is more important to him.

"Right now, George! You've got to do something."

"Uh-huh."

It's no use. Your husband won't respond. You'll have to take matters into your own hands and stop that racket.

Resolutely laying the book down, you head for your daughter's bedroom, up the stairs and to the door. No need to worry that she'll hear you coming.

You open the door. She's seated at the desk with her back to you. Bouncing up and down in the chair, she occasionally uses her pencil. She is doing homework, but you'll never know how. There's the stereo, and there's the plug. Pull it, and tranquility will be restored to your home.

But before you yank that cord, consider your intentions. Does pulling that plug mean your daughter won't listen to rock music elsewhere? Definitely not.

Remember, you allowed those records in your home in the first place. What if your heavy disciplinary hand creates rebellion rather than submission? Wouldn't it be wiser to find out why your daughter likes that music?

We've already discussed the external influence of peer pressure turning kids on to rock. What about the teenage internal craving for rock's beat that is so prevalent in today's young generation? I know how offensive and nerve-wracking that driving, throbbing rock beat is, but, believe it or not, kids really like it.

Before we consider why young people develop an affinity for the rhythm of rock, it's vital that we understand the nature of rock and its musical construction. Irritated parents can't comprehend its power to captivate the body and mind, rendering the mind susceptible to the music's message.

Parents who want to relate to their children by understanding the rock scene must understand the terminology. When you discuss music, teenagers become defensive. They're looking for semantic blunders to negate your opinions of their musical tastes. Calling Phil Collins hard rock (he's not) or assuming that every group lays down primitive, unsophisticated beat patterns (Journey does not) may be the mortal sin that shuts down communication.

It's important that you realize the rhythms may not be objectionable or even classified as rock, although the music sounds raucous to you. For the parent who's ready to pull the plug on his child's stereo, let's explore the world of rock rhythms and delineate some reasonable boundaries.

Many parents are confused about "rock" versus "rock 'n' roll." The term *rock* is an abbreviation of *rock 'n' roll,* but a chronological and musical distinction between these terms has evolved. Though both are used interchangeably, *rock 'n' roll* more precisely refers to pre-1964 sounds or present-day music that emulates the music of artists like Little Richard, Elvis, Bill Haley, Chuck Berry, and the early Beach Boys. It was played mainly by blacks who used pianos and horns, whereas today's rock 'n' roll is primarily performed by small white bands with guitars predominating. Rock 'n' roll is a primitive, loud, and driving musical form that preceded hard rock.

The broadened term *rock* came into journalistic vogue in the late sixties and refers to post-Beatle music. Its definition is less precise and may include the work of such diverse artists as Billy Joel and Eric Clapton. Rock music is more serious, its lyrics more complex than rock 'n' roll. As the product of self-aware musicians, rock is more middle-class than its predecessor, but the terms *rock* and *rock 'n' roll* are used interchangeably by musicians and the record-buying public.

The instrument most closely associated with rock is the guitar. From rock's conception, its rhythmic quality provided the basic sound. Although the unamplified acoustic guitar is used in some softer forms of rock, the electric guitar still dominates. Taking their cue from country and western music, the first rock 'n' roll groups utilized four basic instruments: two guitars for lead and rhythm, a bass, and drums. Toward the end of the fifties, other instruments came into use. Pianos and saxophones became popular, and the dawn of the sixties reverberated with a variety of rock band sounds.

Brass ensembles and string sections with elaborate vocal backing introduced new possibilities. For the first time, full orchestras began performing rock 'n' roll music. Then, late in 1963, the Beatles appeared and started a trend back to small bands, again championing the guitar's basic sound.

During the sixties, there were several brief detours into electronic and orchestral sophistication, but the four- or five-piece rhythm unit reigned supreme. While many groups—notably the Electric Light Orchestra in the seventies and the Eurythmics in the eighties—have made much use of synthesizers, rock is still basically guitar-and-drums music.

Since rock is a hybrid of whole traditions of music—jazz, black spirituals, country and western, blues—there is no typical sound. It became a musical melting pot of many styles revolving around the relentless beat.

This can't be overemphasized. *The focus of rock is the beat.* It is a drummer's holiday. One drummer for a popular rock group beat his drums so hard during performances that doctors ordered his hands bandaged to prevent bleeding.

Despite variations and transitions, rock's essential beat survived. Whatever harmonic, melodic, or verbal sophistication rock may contain, its appeal is its simple, rhythmic, pounding beat.

Mark Farner, legendary lead guitarist for the now-disbanded Grand Funk rock group, once expressed it this way: "I think that now the beat of rock 'n' roll has been driven in. I think that as long as that beat, that feeling, is there—it might not be called rock 'n' roll ten years from now—but it'll be there. That feeling will be there."

Any song can be constructed and performed with a rock format. One aspect of rock is a beat pattern that is incessant and repetitive, achieved by pulsating the rhythm line.

Pulsation is the rhythmic, driving sound most easily associated with rock. It was originally introduced in the early sixties as the West Coast Surfing Sound and consisted of a rapid, throbbing beat. The first pulsation emphasis was upon the guitar and was generated by strumming the lower strings with a successive striking manner. The electric bass became popular and intensified the pulsation of the rhythm guitar and percussion.

A slowed pulsation is usually associated with a "heavy" sound. *Heavy* is a slang adjective that either describes rock (heavy rock) or means something is great. Not all rock is heavy. It is, however, the most basic of the rock sounds and directly related to the rock 'n' roll era. It is heavy in that it trumpets like a herd of charging elephants. The beat is relentless, and it attacks and weighs on the senses with driving insistence.

Rock is not the only music with rhythm, of course. Many early fans of rock find themselves listening to Bach, Haydn, and Mozart in their twenties. Why? Because much classical music, particularly from the Baroque period, has interesting rhythms as well as melodic lines. Jazz has a rhythmic swing. It flows with an exciting, releasing feeling. But heavy metal and hard rock are built from a hard, straight-up-and-down pounding rhythm that produces frustrated energy. Some rock sounds emphasize alternating beats, while other rock tunes hammer every beat home. Though he may add fills (short percussion outbursts), the drummer keeps the force of rock moving with an incessant beat. The listener is enveloped in sound, immersed in the overpowering effect of rock's electronic assault. Rock in its harsher forms doesn't tickle your ears. It rams your skull like a freight train.

An incessantly driving, pulsated beat pattern is not inherently evil, but when applied for a protracted period of time at high volume, it can be hypnotically devastating at live concerts. Like any repetitious assault on one's neurosensory apparatus, it can shut down conscious mental processes. This is the same technique used in Eastern meditative disciplines, like Transcendental Meditation. The result is a heightened suggestibility to images and messages.

That a particular song includes musical pulsation does not signify a negative spiritual potential. But if that pulsation is loud and long enough, the listener may surrender his volitional authority. This is especially true in the case of some heavy metal rock groups whose live performances can rhythmically manipulate an audience until it becomes robotic. In that condition, minds are vulnerable to the message of the music and prey to evil influences.

Pulsated rhythms are not inherently immoral. Their major spiritual concern is the extent to which the beat overrides other musical elements to forces on a basic level of sexual and physical communication.

If rhythms are not evil per se, can they eroticize an audience? This depends on many subjective criteria, such as the moral climate of the concert, the volume level of the sound, the artists' motive, the length of the performance, and whether the listener is sensually vulnerable. There are no definitive guidelines with which to gauge the moral effect of any music. This is a matter that must be judged personally after accounting for all the variables.

Some people automatically designate any repetitive rhythm as morally dangerous, while others naively excuse all rhythms. Both positions are debatable, and neither contributes to understanding problems found in the rock idiom.

Mom and Dad, do you understand now why your child is so caught up in the beat? It's not just noise. It's a carefully constructed rhythm captivating their bodies and capturing their minds. Because of the high-energy world in which you are raising them, they have developed a physiological affinity for the beat.

I know it drives you up the wall and sets your nerves on edge. But they really like it. The same rhythms that repel you, compel them. Because of the addictive nature of rock's rhythm, they can't be easily weaned away. Rock's beat may be potentially destructive under highly selective circumstances (when accompanied by drug usage, when performed at an ear-damaging decibel level at live concerts, when used as an entrancing tool by rock groups involved with the occult). But your main concern should be directed toward what the lyrics say and the singers do.

Don't get hung up on rock's beat. Its musical form is not your biggest problem. You must understand that driving sound for how it envelopes your child's world.

He moves to the sound of a different drummer, and no matter how much you detest it, he likes it. Don't mock it or knock it. That won't get you anywhere. That beat must be replaced by something better suited to healthy moral and musical development. Don't despair. Remember, too, that your child's generation swarmed to see the movie *Amadeus*—and Mozart, the rebellious creator of rhythmic music, may have been the original rock 'n' roller.

TWELVE
DO AS I SAY—AND AS I DO

We've explored how your child is pressured and cajoled into identifying with rock culture, and we have scrutinized youthful responses to rock's music and message. Parents, now it's your turn to be put on the spot.

Perhaps you've tried to discipline your child's musical habits, but he just won't listen. Could your failure stem from a lack of moral authority? Do you contradict yourself?

One reason children ignore instructions regarding musical standards is parental inconsistency. Adult hypocrisy, not a rock conspiracy, can turn kids off to Mom and Dad and on to Billy Idol.

Whenever I challenge teenagers to use discrimination regarding choosing popular music, they immediately present two arguments: "What about the TV programs my parents watch?" and "Their music isn't much better." We'll deal with the first argument in this chapter.

What about it, Mom and Dad? Is your example an asset or a detriment? Can you be honest with yourselves and your children? Let's examine some adult hypocrisies that drive teenagers deeper into the rock culture.

A strong argument against a teen's absorption of the rock culture is his frequent contact with its value system. As a parent, you could overlook the depravity of some rock if it were your child's occasional interest. It isn't. He listens to it constantly. He wakes up to rock on the clock radio, dresses and eats breakfast to it, listens to it on the car radio going to school, takes the Walkman with him during the day, and at night does his homework with the stereo blaring.

Nothing has more pervasive contact with his life, and that bothers you. But confront him about it, and he immediately brings up the many hours you spend watching television. As you consider him propagandized by Prince, he sees you as brainwashed by "Dynasty" and "Dallas."

This indoctrination begins in the living room where television's cesspool pours into the family circle. Programming's voracious appetite for new ideas was sated long ago. Why not violate the forbidden boundaries of sex and violence? Glorification of the sensual has gone beyond adultery to incest and homosexuality, subtly undermining America's morality.

The proliferation of television crime shows based on murder-and-mayhem schools encourages criminally insane values. In some cities, the hand that once reached for candy now holds out a "Saturday Night Special," and a youngster who learned the intricacies of villainy via "Miami Vice" now steals your pocketbook.

Most Christian parents don't attend publicly shown obscene movies. Why bother? Why waste money in a tacky theater when they can hook up to HBO on cable or rent a videocassette and view the same lascivious fare comfortably settled in their own living rooms? A single program may not warp one's mind, but the average family watches television approximately seven hours a day. This relentless bombardment of concepts contrary to Christian values can erode the most firmly entrenched morality.

If television's audiovisual debauchery has a waste dump, it's the afternoon—Mom's prime time to turn on American-style vicarious love fantasies. Soap operas assault Christian standards with morally reprehensible themes. Here are some specific reasons for Christian objection to soaps:

1. *The life-styles presented as normal are concoctions of unregenerate writers who foist their moral foibles on the American housewife.*

In the typical soap household, women are wicked and men are manipulative. Do you know any family that could sustain five affairs, four abortions, three rapes, two suicides, and one attempted case of incest—all in one year? Do you yearn to cheat on your husband, suspect him of sleeping with his secretary, expect to have your teenage daughter turn up pregnant, and plan to slit your wrists in the throes of mental depression? If so, the soaps adequately represent your life. If not, then why subject your family to immoral drama?

2. *Viewers are coerced into identifying with soap characters.*

Viewers cry, laugh, and indulge each emotional trauma as if the actors were real people. Make-believe becomes reality for many soap addicts. Fans have mailed CARE packages to poor soap characters and have bought clothes and champagne to celebrate fictitious weddings. One actress, whose role included a mastectomy resulting from breast cancer, was deluged in real life by letters of condolence. Such empathizing may cause you to rationalize sin, sympathizing with the harried wife who seeks solace in seduction. "After all," you might think, "that tormenting husband drove her to it." Don't underestimate the power of drama to involve the observer morally as well as emotionally.

3. *What you see on television may not seem as repulsive in real life once you have been thoroughly indoctrinated.*

Soaps set trends for America's moral attitude toward life and love. After months of unbridled afternoon lust, the most unsuspecting women may become willing candidates for adultery. If teens' habits are influenced by the rock stars they worship, middle-aged American matrons who idolize soap characters are equally idolatrous toward their matinee heroes, who thrive on deceit and fornication.

Perhaps you think such language is too stern. Could the issue have been presented more gently? Perhaps. But the situation is so serious that major surgery is needed. You're concerned about the music your children listen to. If you are guilty of hypocritical standards concerning the television programs you watch, the point must be made forcefully.

You may argue that one person is powerless over what the networks air. But viewers are to blame. Manufacturers only advertise on television programs with proven ratings, and any effective boycott must begin at the consumer level. Christians are supposed to be the preservative of society, the "salt of the earth" (Matt. 5:13). Can we casually contribute to the rotten viewing habits of millions who don't know the Lord? What about our responsibility to "redeem the time" (Eph. 5:16)? While people seek love and purpose in life, some Christians are more concerned about "The Young and Restless" and "The Days of Our Lives."

Try this experiment. For one week's average viewing schedule, make a list of how many times you are subjected to the following: (1) profanity, (2) the Lord's name used in vain, (3) adultery and fornication portrayed or suggested, (4) murders or attempted murders, (5) verbal and physical assaults, (6) favorable attitudes toward homosexuality, (7) cheating and corner-cutting to get ahead, (8) dirty jokes and lewd remarks, (9) Christianity mocked or attacked, and (10) occult practices glorified or used to instill horror.

The completed list may appall you, but show it to your child and tell him what you plan to do about it. (You will, I hope, decide to carefully monitor future viewing habits in your home.) Ask your child to follow your example. Ask him to compile a similar list based on the music he listens to and the rock stars he admires. With much prayer, his list and your example should resolve the problem of rock's influence on your child's life.

THIRTEEN

WHAT CAN A PARENT DO?

Perhaps your family needs this book. You recognize your children and your home in its pages. You also understand your child's involvement in the rock scene is not only a problem but a symptom. Now, what can you do?

Raising children in today's world requires the understanding of Solomon and the honesty of David. The former was endowed by God with supernatural perception. In the New Testament, James 1:5 promises you the same wisdom. David not only failed, but also acknowledged his shortcomings. Your readiness to do the same is vital toward regaining your child's respect.

Take these three steps immediately to reestablish lines of communication with your children:

1. Be informed.
2. Show love.
3. Set an example.

Part of your shock regarding rock's immorality stems from lack of information. It's surprising how little most parents know about the world of music their children live in. I have waited outside rock concerts and watched cars disgorging teenage occupants. "Have a good time," Mom says as she drives away, dumping her thirteen-year-old daughter into a pot-hazed evening of drugs and titillating sexual innuendo.

Many rock concerts are free zones of drug usage. The atmosphere is so saturated with euphoric odors that one deep breath is nearly enough to get high. Before the first song is played, pot pipes light up. Those who don't come supplied with their own plastic bag full of goodies can easily borrow from a friend. The band onstage exhorts the crowd, "Get high and groove with the sounds." Getting stoned on dope is common at heavy metal rock concerts. With no hassles from the cops to worry about and two hours of high-energy music ahead, tripping out is a part of the reason for being there. What is the reaction of law enforcement authorities? None. To arrest drug offenders would start a riot with serious injuries, and what can be done with five thousand kids after you've arrested them? Imagine the wrath of parents who think their child doesn't use drugs and who believe the police made a mistake!

Why don't more parents know what's going on? Don't they read the newspapers? Can't they smell the sweet odor of pot on their children's clothing? Don't they notice their kids' giddy laughs and spaced-out looks when they get home? Would some parents rather ignore the truth?

Once, while lecturing about rock music in a church, I illustrated my point by showing samples of obscene record albums. One mother vented her frustrations on me. "How dare you disgrace the house of God by showing such trash," she said. "I don't need to know these things."

Her rebuke continued until she stalked off in disgust. The next evening she approached me again. Thinking I was in for another tongue-lashing, I tried to avoid her but she tracked me down.

"I owe you an apology," she said. "When I got home last night, I went straight to my son's room to check out his record collection. To my amazement, I discovered that he had nearly every album you talked about."

She described how she spent the rest of the evening with her son.

"I asked him to go through each album with me and tell me something about each group. At first, he was reluctant. I guess he thought I only wanted to condemn, but after a while he opened up and showed me the lyric sheets. Reading those words was quite a jolt."

She went on. "I did my best not to react self-righteously and, instead, put the burden back on him. I asked questions like, 'Do you really think it's wise to fill your mind with that outlook on life?' and 'Does the image that group presents reflect values which are pleasing to God?' "

Instead of condemning her son's musical tastes, this mother tried to understand his world without being judgmental. She had every reason for concern about the spiritual consequences of his music, but she honestly admitted that her ignorance and oversight had allowed him to purchase those albums in the first place.

"Finally," she continued, "I asked him to play some of the albums for me. I told him not to spare me and pick the worst record he had. He chose Motley Crue. By the time they got through describing quickie sex on an elevator, I thought I'd literally be sick. By the look on my son's face, he wasn't so sure he liked the words either."

"The turning point came," she concluded, "when I confessed to him my failings as a parent. He had never heard that kind of admission from me before. I left his room knowing for the first time I understood a little about the influences in my son's life. He didn't get rid of those records on the spot. That might have been too much to expect. What's more important is that once again I'm talking with my son."

Parents, don't condemn your children's music. They need to know your objections aren't based on a vague dislike for modern forms of musical expression. If you follow the example of the mother just described, you will have taken a courageous step toward reaffirming Christian morality in your child's life.

FOURTEEN
OF COURSE I LOVE MY CHILDREN

Most parents would be offended if love for their children were questioned. To them, their parental affection and devotion are obvious. But do they express their love?

Loving is doing. We devote time and energy to objects of our affection. But don't assume that your child believes you love him just because you provide shelter, clothing, and food. He's part of a welfare state generation that views life's necessities as rights, not privileges, and he may interpret your basic provisions as mere fulfillment of parental obligation.

When was the last time you verbalized affection to your child? You feel it, so why don't you look at your child and say, "I love you"?

My counseling experiences indicate that verbal expressions of love in most homes are sporadic. "I love you" is hard to say because those three words must be based on frequent, open communication. Otherwise, the words are forced and shallow.

During a public appearance, I spoke on the subject of reconciliation in the home. I asked those who needed healing in parent/child relationships to attend a counseling and prayer session. We led everyone to a room and seated them in family units with a circle of chairs facing inward.

Before prayer or teaching, I suggested that each group spend a few moments discussing its problems, hoping some conflicts would be resolved before I offered advice.

The result was revealing. While I waited for each family to begin talking, there was almost total silence. Most just sat there, staring awkwardly at each other. They were obviously uncomfortable, unaccustomed to direct confrontations with family members. I realized why these parents couldn't express love for their children. They couldn't discuss the weather, let alone deeply felt emotions.

Before the counseling session concluded, it was obvious that the conduct in that prayer room represented behavior in the home. Lest you miss the point, let me state it succinctly. Your child may seclude himself with the stereo on full blast because you have nothing to say to him.

For three years I traveled as a professional lecturer representing a secular lyceum agency and a university speakers' bureau, presenting an analysis of America's rock culture. Each lecture began with the following statement: "I could walk out here and ridicule your parents or curse God, and most of you wouldn't do a thing. But if I said one word against your favorite rock group, some of you would tear me limb from limb."

Almost without exception that remark would be met with retorts of "You bet!" or "Right on!" or "You'd better believe it!"

Why? Because rock is more than a form of music to the teenager. It is a way of life that consumes his every waking moment. Rock musicians mean more than his parents because they have become a surrogate family. You may say "I love you" occasionally to him, but so do his rock stars.

You might respond defensively, "Sure, but the love in rock songs is cheap affection that's only expressed to eroticize young people and get their money. You don't suppose my daughter thinks those guys in the posters on her wall really love her?"

Probably not. But in the absence of your affection and open communication, that may not be apparent to your child.

While counseling teenagers, I often asked this question: "If you had serious personal problems, to whom would you go for advice?"

The list of prospects included friends, school counselors, clergy, even casual acquaintances. In fact, teenagers discussed with me things they have never told their parents. That's tragic. Parents should be the first resort in times of need. Their counsel should be sought constantly.

Why don't parents top the list? Moms and dads should ask themselves these questions:

"Am I too busy to spend time with my children?"

"Am I aware of what's going on in their world?"

"Can they talk freely with me about anything at any time?"

"Do they know that I really love them, and do I tell them so?"

If your answer to any of these questions is no, you have some clues about the lack of communication with your child. Stop for a moment and listen to the songs they're hearing. Their rock heroes are saying, "We understand your problems. We care about you. Get high with us. We've got the answers."

Though false, they hear that message all day long and are convinced of its veracity. Your child may know deep inside that you love him and care about his welfare. But unless you tell him what you feel, it won't do much good.

A final word of caution. When you express love, base it on who your child is, not on what he's done. Affection expressed because of achievement is hollow. God may not have blessed you with a quarterback or a cheerleader. Don't wait until your kid comes home with all A's on his report card to say, "We're proud of you."

Young people see through phony affection. They know when Mom and Dad want them to excel because of personal pride. The rock scene accepts them as they are—dirty jeans, bad grades, adolescent frustrations, and all. When you indicate acceptance is based on accomplishment, a rock singer may sound far more honest. That's why his poster is on your child's wall.

Praise the successes of your children, but also understand their failures. Perhaps their expertise isn't what you planned. It's frustrating to be the child of a father who likes to hunt and fish if your interests are in art and music. Expect the best of them, and teach them to strive for excellence. But don't let your pride or expectations exceed the gifts and abilities God gave them.

Love them because they're yours, God's gift of life, and you'll always be number one in their eyes. More important, they won't question your love for them.

FIFTEEN

WHAT ABOUT *YOUR* MUSIC?

Nearly every youngster is convinced his dad is a superman and his mother is marvelous. Part of growing up is discovering mother may not be the world's most beautiful woman, and father is not the strongest man this side of Atlas.

There's a bit of child in all of us. My dad is seventy-eight years old, and I still think there are things nobody can do as well as he can. No one can bake a pie as good as my mom's. There are many great people I admire, but my parents are still my heroes. And they always will be.

They aren't perfect. I've been around long enough to see the chinks in their armor. But God told me to honor them and gave me the innate capacity to do so. Their example has earned that respect. They've seen their ups and downs. I've watched their bouts with disappointment and sickness. But their faith in God today is stronger than ever.

God doesn't make perfect parents. He commands them to set an example, a model that will include error. But there is no excuse for irresponsible, hypocritical inconsistencies that can be avoided by honesty and commitment to Christ.

One evening I sat in the home of a wealthy South American businessman in Bogota, Colombia, a city that is a major supplier of drugs to North America. His observations were revealing.

"Visit our jails," he said, "and you'll find few Colombian youth there. Those arrested for drugs are mostly Americans. Our children are taught never to touch drugs. Valium is available over the counter without a prescription. Still, good Colombian parents won't touch it. To take tranquilizers would be a hypocritical example. How, then, could we tell our children not to take drugs?"

Your children want to follow your example. Give them something to aim for.

Incidents of adult hypocrisy are many, but there's one topic teenagers bring up frequently when their parents knock rock. The symbol of inconsistency that bugs them is the music that so many Bible-belt, middle-American adults favor—country and western.

Most adults are stunned when they learn the lyrics of the rock tunes their children listen to. Why have they never noticed the words of their favorite country songs? Let the preacher knock rock, and Dad shouts, "Amen!" After the service, he gets in his car, tunes to the country station, and all the way home listens to songs about truck drivers who shack up with waitresses or go to honky-tonks to drown their sorrows in booze. Rich Blackburn, general manager of CBS Records in Nashville, says, "I'm chasing the thirty-year-old who drives a Blazer, drinks beer, frequents movies, and likes Hank Williams, Jr."

Triangle-affair songs and casual adultery lubricated with liquor provide the main subject matter. Which is worse, AC/DC singing, "Lickin' off the sweat on her favorite trick" ("Shake Your Foundations") or Conway Twitty declaring, "We've never been this far before"? The Rolling Stones may not be paragons of moral virtue, but are they any worse than erotically enhanced Dolly Parton or "outlaw" oriented, pot-smoking Willie Nelson? Rock entertainers' promiscuous escapades may horrify Mom, but why does she buy the records of multiple divorcee Tammy Wynette? Is the erotic performance of the Eurythmics' Annie Lennox really any worse than country artist Barbara Mandrell singing, "Married, but not to each other"?

The frankness and titillating explicitness of country songs is embarrassing. "With your blouse halfway open," sings Tommy Overstreet, "don't go city on me." In "Cheap Perfume and Candlelight," Bobby Borchers tells his lover that, if she can't make it at home, to make it any way she can. David Houston sings of the "No Tell Motel" ("We're here all night . . . cheatin' has become our way of life"). Johnny Duncan gets right to the point when he declares, "She can put her shoes under my bed anytime." Other memorable country and western lines include: "I'd make love to you in a New York minute, and take my Texas time doin' it."

Female artists respond with equal bluntness. One song says, "Lord, I am a Christian but I am a woman too." Sammi Smith sings, "I'll let you touch me," but adds, "It just won't feel like cheating with you." "Soft Lights and Slow Sexy Music" are recommended by Jody Miller. Jeannie Seely leaves nothing to the imagination by suggesting, "Take me to bed (and I'll be good)." Today's female country singers have punctured the God-fearing, powder-puff image of the past with lines like "The door is always open, and the light's on in the hall." Chastity is a detriment to the image of some country music-singing gals.

Among female country singers, fashionable and sexy clothing is a means of feminine expression, with Madonna-like maidens populating the country caravans. Country music has come a long way since Loretta Lynn's birth control anthem "The Pill" was banned on country stations in 1975. Perhaps female country artists should be reminded of the Kitty Wells' rejoinder, "It wasn't God who made honky-tonk angels."

If there are diehard country fans among the parents reading this book, check out the titles of some recent hits: "I Love That Woman Like the Devil Loves Sin," "It's All Wrong but It's All Right," "What Did I Promise Her Last Night," "Bedroom Eyes," "Would You Lay with Me in a Field of Stone," "Wake Up on the Warm Side of You," "I Cheated on a Good Woman's Love," "When the Fire Gets Hot," "It's a Cheating Situation," "I Just Can't Stay Married to You," "Do You Ever Fool Around," "Put Your Clothes Back On," "Undercover Lover," "I Never Made Love Till I Made It with You," "Unwed Fathers," and "If I Said You Had a Beautiful Body, Would You Hold It against Me"?

What disturbs young people most is the veneer of religious hypocrisy that glosses over the country music scene. Some country artists sing the praises of stolen love one minute and switch to "Amazing Grace" the next. Two of the biggest country hits, "Heaven's Just a Sin Away" and "It Don't Feel Like Sinnin' to Me," were recorded by singers who claim to be staunch church members. Other country lines concerning religion include: "If Heaven ain't like Dixie, then I don't want to go;" "I've got some crazy friends who forgive me of my sin"; "Jesus loves me this I know, so I just keep rollin' with the flow." Christian artists like Ricky Skaggs carry their faith into their songs and avoid the cheating-is-a-way-of-life theme, but such artists are in the minority. Is it any wonder your child wants you to clean up your own backyard before trampling on his?

If we dropped the subject now, enough might have been said to convince the antirock, procountry music fan of his double standard. But sex isn't country music's only subject. Topic number two is alcohol.

Songs praising booze include "Red Wine and Blue Memories," "Two More Bottles of Wine," "Whiskey Trip," "The Power of Positive Drinking," "Heaven Was a Drink of Wine," and "Bartender Blues."

Substance abuse is also a part of country stars' life-styles. Waylon Jennings admits he was seriously addicted to cocaine and claims that his album *Turn the Page* was the first record in twenty years he recorded without the assistance of drugs. Several years ago, George Jones was arrested for driving ninety-one miles per hour, and he was charged with public drunkenness and cocaine possession. Willie Nelson caused a controversy during the Carter presidency when he and his band, invited to perform at the White House, told reporters that the band did *not* perform unless they had smoked pot first. While country music concerts are not the pot-hazed affairs that many rock concerts are, few country stars try to model drug-free, booze-free living.

Country music isn't always as pro-American, pro-establishment as many people think. Parents who loudly denounce the anti-establishment ways of rock groups cheer wildly as Johnny Paycheck sings "Take This Job and Shove It." In the tune "Morning Desire," Kenny Rogers decides to stay home and make love to the woman he is in bed with and contemplates lying to his employer.

Remember when you were a kid? Floyd Tillman sang of promiscuously "Slipping Around" and Hank Thompson declared "Swing Wide Your Gates of Love." You'll have to admit that country music hasn't gotten better. Sure, there are train songs, homesick songs, and God-bless-America songs. But they're not in the majority.

Conway Twitty, a major country star, reflected on his years as an entertainer and said, "As a country artist, I'm not proud of a lot of things in my field. There is no doubt in my mind that we are contributing to the moral decline in America."[1] *Music* magazine described a Twitty concert this way: "When he sings 'As My Trembling

Fingers Touch Forbidden Places,' the hall erupts with squeals and screams. It's a moment of good, clean family fun. After all, it's only make-believe.''

What is the attitude of the country music industry? The vice president of Elektra Records in Nashville says, "Music is a mirror of the times. If country music has become smutty, then America has probably become smuttier, too.'' A record executive for Warner Brothers argues, "There may be some suggestive lines from time to time, but country music reflects real emotions and genuine situations.''

Enough said? Probably. It's always easier to trample on the kids' toes than on Dad's. But before we drop this subject, permit me to share the words of a poem I wrote about country music. Then, we'll let the matter land on your doorstep, Mom and Dad, while your children watch to see how you pick it up.

The Country and Western Song

Merle, Buck and Porter, Waylon, Willie, Dolly too,
Sing truck drivin', drinkin' tunes and songs to make you blue.
Honky-tonkin' angels aren't the kind you'll meet some day;
If I may correct their song, "Hell's just a sin away."

Triangle affair songs always take the biggest part,
All the time it seems that someone's breakin' someone's heart.
If those singers really lived those songs they'd most be dead
From exhaustion getting in and out of all those beds.

Country-Western music doesn't have a sexy beat;
It's not like that rock 'n' roll to get you on your feet.
Parents tell their kids the Rolling Stones they shouldn't hear,
But those country music words would burn a sailor's ears.

All they sing about is just unhappiness and strife,
And how someone's sleepin' with somebody else's wife.
But before they close the show and bid you all good-night,
They toss in a hymn of faith to make it seem all right.

I'll admit that country singers don't have freaky hair;
Okies from Muskogee don't snort cocaine everywhere.
They're not like those rock stars who take drugs to get along;
They're just drunk on liquor while they sing those truckin' songs.

Someday when your death has come and you have said good-bye,
Then I wonder if you'll see a jukebox in the sky,
Filled with all the country songs you've heard along the way,
To check out where you belong when it comes to Judgment Day.[2]

NOTES
1. *People*, September 3, 1979, p. 82.   2. Bob Larson, copyright 1978, used by permission.

SIXTEEN
A RECORD-BREAKING EVENT

Dear Mr. Larson,

I'm writing to tell you of an important decision I just made. Last night I broke all my rock albums that I felt were hindering my Christian life. I feel so good inside. For the first time, I am really free to serve the Lord.

It wasn't easy to do. In fact, the first time I read your book, it made me so mad I threw it across the room. But what you said stayed with me, and I started watching to see how my life was influenced by the music I heard.

You were right. I began to notice myself accepting more tolerant attitudes toward sex and drugs. My music was gradually brainwashing me until I almost quit serving the Lord completely.

I only wish other teenagers like me could know the joy that comes from making a full commitment to Christ. Please pray for me that I can stick by my decision.

Sincerely,
Randy

As a parent, you're probably wishing Randy were your son. You'd like your son or daughter to make that decision, because you're concerned about the music they listen to. If only they could see the damage it's doing and break their offensive albums like Randy did.

Realistically, that's probably wishful thinking. It would be great if they made that decision on their own, but for several reasons it's unlikely.

For one thing, teenagers who indiscriminately listen to rock can find plenty of support from other Christians. When you question your child's listening habits, he can readily muster help from respected Christian leaders who claim teens shouldn't worry about involvement in the rock scene.

A popular Christian youth periodical reviews secular rock albums on a monthly basis. Its glowing endorsements have included records by many of the bands I've mentioned in this book.

"But how," you ask, "could a conscientious Christian feel comfortable supporting singers whose lives represent the antithesis of Christian behavior?"

Many Christian parents were raised in a restrictive age. What may be called "legalism" or "holiness" today was normal Christian conduct thirty years ago. Christians just didn't do some things. No questions were asked. If Mom or the pastor said no, that was reason enough. Today's Christian young people have a different perspective. To understand their more lenient life-style, you must know about certain contemporary Christian philosophies.

"Christian" dances are increasingly popular in some circles. A secular periodical visited such dance halls and found hundreds of young people "boogying to the discs of gospel artists."[1] One $350,000 teen disco features two dance floors, laser strobes, and a $35,000 sound system.

Wake up, Mom and Dad. It's a new world. The old taboos are falling fast. Formerly restricted behavior has become accepted conduct. You need to examine the rationale behind these trends.

Of course, Christians should avoid an entertainer who glorifies debauchery. You're probably perplexed that anyone could consider the erotic gesticulations accompanying rock dancing a form of spiritual expression. Your wildest imagination couldn't conceive that Christ is honored by flashing lights, a throbbing beat, and undulating bodies.

But to some contemporary Christians, these apprehensions are irrelevant. They believe each person controls his own spiritual condition, regardless of negative outside influences. Teenagers are told that the media represents little threat to the Christian and that music is a minor factor in the larger context of life.

As a Christian periodical put it, "Sometimes rock turns ugly when it shows us our own ugliness—but it should not be censored because of that. Sometimes we need to see ourselves as we really are."[2]

That perspective places undue stress on the discerning faculties of human nature. It's more realistic to acknowledge that, while the spirit may be willing, the flesh is weak. That's why we are told in the Bible to "come out" from the world's value system and not wallow in its warped philosophies.

Some adults possess the character and spiritual stability to withstand an onslaught of satanic ideologies, but a youngster in the throes of adolescence is not likely to remain unscathed. He is going through a developmental stage of life where moral values are formed. Is it safe to assume he will be unimpressed by the ideas and imagery of his entertainment heroes?

It may be easy for an evangelical journalist to shoot from the lip and give teenagers the benefit of the doubt. But as a parent, you know the frailty of a young person's ability to resist cultural pressure. You want your child protected against the objectionable songs that have been outlined in this book. You'd probably feel better if your son would break his rock albums like Randy did.

But what would he listen to then? That's what the next chapter is all about.

NOTES
1. *Billboard*, December 18, 1976.   2. *Campus Life*, December 1978.

S E V E N T E E N
FILLING THE VACUUM

"But there's nothing else to listen to!"

That emotional defense is typical after suggesting that a young person diminish his steady diet of rock music. He has never learned to understand other kinds of music, and his artistic appreciation is stunted. Taking away rock removes an emotional security blanket that leaves some teenage lives in a musical vacuum.

Most teenagers have little interest in the classics and are bored by the middle-of-the-road pop sounds. But they do crave music. It's part of their upbringing, and the thought of going through life without sound and rhythm is a dismal prospect.

That's a sad commentary on our culture. We are constantly massaged by sound. Nearly every home has a stereo or television on constantly. Our cars are equipped with tape decks. Stores and restaurants ply their wares with subliminal sound, and most offices and factories program music to increase productivity.

Modern man feels naked without sound to soothe his day, and Christian teenagers are victims of this syndrome. They aren't quite comfortable in a quiet environment. Is it any wonder they have difficulty establishing a faith that will sustain them? The Bible tells us that only by being still shall we truly come to know God.

There's little comfort in lamenting our modern life-style. We're all part of it, like it or not. Though we may find occasional solitary times of quietness and hear God speak, we must function in the real world, enveloped in music.

Do we fight the younger generation's affinity for musical surroundings or take advantage of it? Fighting is impossible unless you plan to pack up your family and move to the Hindu Kush. How can we turn to good that which was meant for evil?

There is a simple answer. Show young people there is something else to listen to, Christian music that speaks to them in an acceptable, enjoyable idiom. Contemporary Christian music has experienced a dramatic upheaval resulting in a diversity of recorded sounds to inspire faith, to minister to deep needs, and to simply enjoy.

Not all of these developments have been positive, and there have been rough spots along the way. In the early seventies, the Jesus Revolution spawned a new generation of singers, songwriters, and musicians who sang about their Savior so peers could understand. Instead of solemnly warbling to the accompaniment of an organ and piano, they plugged in their guitars and set the drums beating.

Overzealousness and naivete dominated their early efforts. Anything that had the name of Jesus tacked on was regarded as positive. When George Harrison extolled Hinduism in "My Sweet Lord" and Jewish singer Norman Greenbaum unscripturally spoke of Christ as a "Spirit in the Sky," few cared. It didn't matter that Jesus was being portrayed as a confused and doubting revolutionary in *Jesus Christ Superstar* and an imbecilic clown in *Godspell*. At least he was being discussed.

While such secular rip-offs were praised, church resistance to those first new sounds was often met with belligerence. Those who counseled caution were countered with pious pragmatism. "If it brings souls to Jesus," critics were told, "the results justify the means."

A new day of church music was dawning, but the change came too abruptly for most Christian leaders. Many were concerned that a philosophy of expediency was being pursued too uncritically. Such objections were often met with a hipper-than-thou attitude.

"If the church won't bend," many musicians concluded, "we'll just roll right over it."

Roll they did, rocking all the way. When adults who were nurtured on George Beverly Shea expressed shock, they were told, "Why should the devil have all the good music?" Words like *relate* and *communicate* became sacred cows. Few cared about the musical form used to present Christ. Telling people about him was the goal, and how it was done mattered little.

The world's sounds and jargon were mimicked in a mixture of entertainment and evangelism. "If Luther borrowed from his culture," many asked, "why not assimilate ours and reflect it in a Christian context?" But, unlike the Reformer who extracted most of his songs on a level of excellence, these guitar-toting minstrels tended to gravitate to the lower denominator of pop culture.

In spite of their sincerity, these young musicians marked the early days of contemporary Christian music with a shallow side of Christian life. Sometimes the lyrics were too subjective and ambiguous. Authentic, contemporary Christian expression was hard to find. Secular trends were copied without originality.

Whatever reservations may have been expressed regarding this new musical awakening, one thing was clear. The church was feeling the reverberations of the secular realm where virtually the entire music industry consisted of people under thirty. For the first time, control of Christian musical expression had escaped adult leadership.

Teenagers were no longer quietly subservient to their elders' musical tastes. They now had their own music, regardless of its frivolity. At least they were no longer bored by the unrelenting diet of outdated anthems and hymns.

As the beat of contemporary Christian music grew louder and stronger, dissenting voices were raised, mine among them. I saw something disturbing in the defiant rejection of biblical guidelines for musical expression. A poor imitation of the world's music and life-styles was not the way to reach sin-sick kids who were looking for a way out. Musically endorsing their frustrations could not lift them to Christ's level. Much of the music catered to their immature musical tastes with a false perspective on Christian living that ignored the sacrifice of the Cross.

I saw no hope that spiritually viable musical expression could evolve from confusion. It seemed impossible that these Christian rock artists would ever mellow and mature into composers and singers who would explore themes of depth and commitment worthy of acceptance by the church. But I was wrong!

I made another miscalculation. I, too, was part of a generation looking for new ways to make known the name of Jesus. My reservations and objections were designed to purify, not stifle. But I seriously underestimated the prejudiced inertia of the evangelical church.

I was shocked that my cautious views were taken further than intended. What I had written and said was used by certain church leaders to turn thumbs down on anything that smacked of being "contemporary." The mere sight of guitars and drums in God's house was considered a pollution of the sanctuary.

As a critic, I carefully thought through my apprehensions. I strongly wished that young people would develop an honest form of musical expression. I voiced strong objections to the spiritual superficiality around me. I learned too late that many parents endorsed my cautions out of prejudice, not empathy.

But while I was expressing concerns about the direction of Christian music, many adults prepared for war. The contemporary sounds of the seventies were declared a battleground upon which faith itself was disputed. Parents were at odds with their children, who couldn't understand what all the fuss was about.

Instead of pointing out the shallow and commending the good, many church leaders dug in their heels for a fight to the finish. Conflict raged between those who wanted unrestricted musical expression and those determined to venerate the past. All the while, the guitars kept right on strumming and the tunes kept right on coming.

Today, the evangelical church has entered a new era. Records and tapes are the fastest growing aspect of the Christian bookseller industry. Many stores report that 50 percent of their sales volume is contemporary Christian music.

The airwaves are filled with it. In the United States, over twenty-five hundred stations program some Christian music. Many Christian stations have devoted entire formats to contemporary sounds. Top-forty Christian music charts now list the current popularity of the latest releases. It's significant that not long ago there weren't enough albums recorded to devise a chart.

Christian music is big business. People like Amy Grant, Russ Taff, Petra, and Phil Keaggy—to mention a few—produce albums that compete commercially in the secular marketplace. Jesus festivals draw thousands of people to gatherings reminiscent of the old brush arbors. Uplift is combined with outreach to feature Bible teachers and high-energy music. Like mini-Woodstocks (minus the sex and drugs), these happenings have made Jesus cheers as common as "How Great Thou Art." Not everyone is happy about these developments, but no one can deny that the church has changed and music is leading the way. Parents cannot ignore those amplified sounds and condemn them as an obnoxious fad. The clock doesn't turn backwards, so parents must understand what is happening and plan for the future.

The vacuum is being filled. Christian young people who forsake the degenerate sounds of secular rock have an option. Their local Christian bookstore has stacks of albums by contemporary artists whose musical expression reflects youthful thinking. Adolescent feelings are explored with perceptive and challenging lyrics. Parents, don't get hung up on the emotional impact of words like *rock*. Much of what goes under the heading of "Christian rock" bears little resemblance to the shallow, secular, early seventies raucous rock.

Of course, not all trends in the contemporary Christian music scene are positive and praiseworthy. But even the worst modern attempts at expressing Christian faith are better than the secular sex-drenched paeans to hedonism. But beware lest the teenager, rebounding from the unregenerate world of rock, "jumps out of the frying pan. . . ."

EIGHTEEN
INTO THE FIRE

But some of that Christian music doesn't sound any different than the secular rock my children listen to now.

From a musical standpoint, you may be right.

Well, then, what good will it do to encourage them to buy contemporary Christian music records?

The lyrics of the songs won't be saturated with immorality. The musicians have given their talents to the Lord. Most are genuinely concerned about lifting up Jesus, not glorifying the satyric life that preoccupies so much of secular rock.

Are all Christian rock musicians like that? I've heard that some groups are just as egocentric as the secular ones. They seem to be as concerned about the commercial success of their music as unsaved entertainers.

Some of them are. That's a serious problem, but don't let the antics of a few groups color your thinking about all contemporary Christian artists.

Well, I'll concede that most of them are probably sincere. They exhibit a Christian testimony, and their lyrics focus on Jesus. But the music is still the same. It's got that THUMP-THUMP beat.

A lot of the songs do. Some musicians lay down a beat as heavy as anything ever churned out by Bon Jovi. There is even a Christian heavy metal band, Stryper, and their music—though not their lyrics—is as "heavy" as any secular group's. But this isn't typical of most contemporary Christian music.

I'm confused. All that music sounds alike to me.

That's part of the problem. Most adults are unaware of the wide variety of contemporary pop sounds. Teenagers often have a stunted sense of musical appreciation, but some parents cannot understand the diversity of both secular and contemporary Christian music. Just as their children categorize Mom's music as "slow and boring," Mom is critical of unfamiliar harmonies and rhythms.

Contemporary Christian music is young and growing. It has many shortcomings, and some inconsistencies are too apparent. Remember, these zealous musicians are filled with youthful idealism. Their impetuousness sometimes gets the best of them, and short-range goals overpower other concerns. Maturity has a way of mellowing the most fervent zealot, but most young musicians haven't had the chance to view their art from a historical perspective.

I agree with all that. But the beat still bothers me.

Your concern is legitimate. But be cautious. The subject requires total honesty from you as a parent.

There's no way to analyze the subject of Christian music and define its scope and limitations in a way that will satisfy everyone. We're all unique with divergent cultural backgrounds. That makes life exciting. Your likes and dislikes are a product of God's special way of forming life. Sameness stifles, while diversity enriches.

Because music is a form of individual and cultural expression, there is no consensus. One Sunday morning in India, I spoke to a group of Tamil Indian Christians whose song service was a shock to my system. The banging of drums mingling with a variety of cymbals and untuned guitars was cacophonous, but their smiles radiated a love for Christ that transcended our dissimilar tastes.

Do you enjoy anthems, solemnity, and pipe organ preludes? Do they epitomize an atmosphere of worship? That's fine, but don't try to impose your evaluation on a black congregation in the Caribbean. I've watched them sing and sway with an enthusiasm that would bring an infectious smile to all but the most somber deacon.

God can't be boxed. Try it, and he breaks out to inspire those in his body who are willing to respond spontaneously to the Spirit. Creativity is a gift from God, and who can say how the Lord will channel that gift? Nearly every preacher who has said God wouldn't or couldn't has later had to eat his words or retrench into a legalistic fortress.

Am I suggesting that anything goes? No, but I do counsel a discerning and compassionate approach to this volatile subject of what perimeters apply to Christian music. There are no neatly structured boxes providing absolute guidelines.

It would be easier if there was a formula to go by. Any Christian music that fit the formula would be permissible for your children and taboo if not. Rather than seeking simplistic musical guidelines, why not ask some more basic questions:

Why does music exist? Who is the source of music? What is its purpose for mankind and the church?

Satan may lay claim to using music for the widest extent of expression and effect, but he didn't write the first song. Music sprang from the heart of God, who gave this gift to man for his pleasure and enrichment. When we see the handiwork of God and experience his love in our own lives, we have no right to be silent. God fashioned our lips and lungs to sing forth praises and thanksgiving to him. Our hands have been endowed with the ability to construct instruments upon which melody is created to harmonize with the song of creation.

The Bible records many times when God's people burst forth with music to honor exploits of the Lord. When the Israelites crossed the Red Sea, they sang of their deliverance. In the Psalms, David set to music the joys and anguish of his heart. It was he who arranged for thousands of musicians to accompany the Ark of the Lord. The sound of it all must have been magnificent as the singers blended with psalteries, trumpets, harps, and cymbals. David's song of 1 Chronicles 16 exemplifies how music can be a declaration of faith as well as an expression of joy.

When Jesus came into the world, God chose music to reach man's heart. The Lord's birth was made known by a chorus of angels who serenaded simple shepherds. That nocturnal declaration fulfilled the prophecy of the Magnificat sung by the Virgin Mary to magnify the Lord.

The New Testament records that singing filled the hearts of believers who had found their Messiah. God shook a prison when Paul and Silas sang. Ephesians 5:19 and Colossians 3:16 make it obvious that music was soon incorporated into Christian worship gatherings. "Is any merry?" the apostle James asked, "let him sing psalms." The most glorious anticipation of the Church is to join the saints of the ages in a great songfest. The psalmist spoke in Psalms 40:3 and 98:1 of a "new song" to consummate his faith.

Jehoshaphat sent forth musicians to precede and proclaim the victory of the Lord as he stood still to see God's salvation. It is only fitting that Christians who now await God's final triumph should burst forth with song. Our salvation is also soon to be revealed when we shall gather around the throne of God. Our "new song" in that day, described in Revelation 5:9, will be an unending anthem of praise to our Savior.

But the new song of the Lord is not yet a clarion melody to our world. Satan too often infiltrates its purity with his old song. We must abhor the devil's music with an intensity equal to our appreciation of the Lord's song.

While it is clear that God is the source of music, Ezekiel 28:13 implies that Satan was the first musician. But his song, which once resounded about God's throne, turned into a dirge of death when he rebelled against the Almighty. Since that day, the devil has had the world dancing to his tune.

Like every gift of God, music has often been perverted to serve Satan's ends. He who, before his fall, played the song of the Lord on harp and pipes, later skillfully constructed sounds to facilitate the worship of those evil angels who rebelled with him. Even God's own people have listened to the "sound of the viol" until the Lord declared, "Take away from me the noise of your songs" (Amos 5:23; 6:5).

But though entire nations could be deceived into bowing before Satan's sounds, God always found men whose ears were tuned to the Lord's melody. Shadrach, Meshach, and Abednego refused to heed the tune of the cornet, flute, harp, sackbut, psaltery, and dulcimer. They were not offended by the tones, harmonies, and rhythms of these instruments. (The Lord himself sanctions the sound of these musical inventions elsewhere in his Word.) It was the motive that mattered, not the music.

Their refusal was not based on rejecting the virtuosity, talent, performance, and melodic construction of music. A fiery furnace was hardly worth facing for a mere difference over musical tastes. What they did count sufficient for not heeding the musical supplication was the pagan purpose behind it. This is the lesson we must observe.

It is not the rhythmic aspects of a musical composition that render it good or evil. When music is truly directed toward the glorification of God, it becomes a valuable asset to inspire faith. But a song that only lifts up the singer is too egocentric for Christian worship or evangelism.

I have had the privilege of traveling to more than seventy countries around the globe. As a student of world religions, I have observed that no religion outside of Christianity has so generously incorporated music as a means of expression. Even the heathen and agnostic must admit that some of the greatest music in human history owes a debt of inspiration to the Christian faith.

I have walked among Hindus, Taoists, Buddhists, Muslims, and other devotees of major religions. While music does play a minor role in their worship and devotion, there is nothing to compare with the centrality of music to Christianity. The reason seems apparent. Faith in Christ is devoid of appeasement and ritual. Love for our Savior ushers forth with such spontaneity and exuberance that the true believer must sing.

What kind of song should we sing? Does the character and quality of Christian music play a role in determining its effect?

It seems axiomatic that music about God should be like God. His beauty, love, harmony, consistency, mercy, peace, and graciousness should be part of our songs. Not every tune needs to embody all the attributes of God. There is room for subjective expression of one's personal view of faith as well as more colloquial statements. But there is one stringent rule: The lyrics should never depart from scriptural suppositions that direct people to thoughts about God's works and ways.

What of the music itself? Are there appropriate guidelines for musical structure? Obviously, lyrics are the first consideration. But if the content is consistent with the principles we've already considered, do the melody and rhythm need to be scrutinized for deficiencies? Let's return to our axiom: Music about God should be like God. How does that apply to a contemporary Christian group with amplified instruments and a decibel capacity to blast out rhythmically pulsating sounds?

A group that plays to lift up Jesus will not concentrate on mere showmanship to entertain its audience, which doesn't mean that mellow acoustics are more spiritually viable. There are times when God speaks his Word with volume and intensity. One can only wonder what would happen in some sedate church gatherings if someone were to take seriously the psalmist's suggestion to "Praise him upon the loud cymbals!"

Some evangelicals have a real hang-up regarding drums. Immediately after my conversion from the world of rock music, I did too, but the Lord soon shattered my prejudice. I was privileged to hear a drum solo performed by a newly converted jazz musician. To the accompaniment of Scripture reading, he audibly demonstrated God's great attributes.

When God thundered, his bass drum nearly burst. The cadence of his snare brought forth visions of the marching armies of heaven. As God descended on Sinai in power and majesty, he launched into a flurry of rolls and cymbal crashes. At the conclusion, I was breathless. What many would consider "the devil's instrument" had ushered me into the presence of God and destroyed my bias.

Christian music should touch the head and the heart. When it only appeals to the hip and the heel, the spiritual benefit suffers. The rhythm of a song should carry, not constrict, the words. Music about Jesus should honor the gentleness of the Holy Spirit, not force itself by the power of its beat. The problem with such cautions is that they tend to be filtered through prejudices. Some musicians find them too restrictive, while many adults will apply them with conservative vengeance.

Perhaps differences of interpretation lie not so much in musical tastes as in the lack of true spiritual discernment among Christians. Man is a trichotomous being—body, soul (mind-consciousness), and spirit. Many times, what is presumed spiritual is actually of the soul. Some young people at Christian concerts boogie and bounce with abandon to the beat and exclaim, "Couldn't you feel the Spirit?"

A musically induced high is too often assumed to be a spiritual experience. That which arouses the body and soul may not contribute to the edification of the spirit. It's not wrong that music makes you feel good. There is nothing wrong if the body responds to a catchy rhythm. But it may be erroneous to equate the effects with a spirit-enriching encounter.

Where does this leave you when walking into a Christian bookstore to buy a contemporary record album? First, you should be excited to find the wide variety. Secondly, you should buy an album that will contribute spiritually through its music and message. Don't buy a Christian record on the same merits you would purchase a secular album. Certainly the quality of the arrangements will be a deciding factor. But if the commercial viability of a record's sound is your only purpose in buying it, you have only jumped out of the frying pan into the fire.

NINETEEN
THANKS, MOM AND DAD

So far, this has been a book about children for parents. We looked at communication problems in the home. Parents' responsibility to express love and set examples has been seen as one way to resolve family differences. But teenagers also have an obligation in the process of healing.

After you finish reading this book, pass it on to your children. This chapter approaches them with a question: "When was the last time you said thanks to Mom and Dad?"

Your generation is the most materialistic in history. Former luxuries are now commonplace. Our affluent philosophy has supported the idea that life's necessities are a right. Food and shelter are bare minimums. While former generations survived with few pleasures, people today worry about "the quality of life," meaning a life with as many material possessions as possible.

Average young people expect easy access to life's necessities. The roof over their heads, the food in their stomachs, and the clothes on their backs are given only cursory thought. The toil their parents endure to make life easy is rarely acknowledged. Why are frequent expressions of gratitude necessary? After all, that's what parents are for!

Do you know your parents love you more than anything in the world? Some parents may be self-centered exceptions, but I haven't met many of them. Most of the parents I've talked to would literally die for their children.

They cared for you with pain and sacrifice. You don't remember the dirty diapers, the sleepless hours from midnight walks, and the bouts with childhood diseases. But they do. Your parents know the labor of love it took to raise you from babyhood through childhood to adolescence.

Mom and Dad watched you spill food as you insisted on using your own spoon. They gingerly launched you on your first steps and soothed the hurt when you stumbled. They saw you pass puberty and emerge with your own sexual identity. Your love for them along the way made all the heartache and denial worth it.

You were dependent upon your parents, but something happened when you became a teenager. Now you want to make your own decisions. That's good. It shows you have matured enough to develop your own value system. Mom and Dad have to learn now which apron strings to cut and which to keep.

You have become your own person, not quite equal to your parents, but a separate identity with your own emotions and opinions. Before, expressions of love to your mom and dad came naturally. Thanking them for special things was easy.

Now things are different. Your elders' values and restrictions often conflict with yours. As a child, you were expected to obey without question. Today, you want answers and reasons. "No" is not good enough. You also want to know why.

God planned this stage of your life beautifully. He knows you must learn to defend your own convictions. Mom and Dad won't always be around to protect and shelter you, and it's necessary that you establish your own personality. But be careful! Don't forget your parents' continuing importance, and don't ignore how much they need to know you still need them.

All this boils down to the question: When was the last time you expressed gratitude to your parents?

Have you said thanks to them lately for the basics of life and the extra pleasures they provide? Why not go to them right now and say something like this:

"Dad, I know you work hard to support our family. You put in long hours so we can have a place to live and food to eat. Sometimes I take these things for granted. But I want you to know I do appreciate all you do for us. Thanks, Dad."

"Mom, you always make sure there's a meal on the table. You even try to bake a special treat when you can. You're always doing what you can to make our house a home. We'd be in a mess without you. Thanks, Mom."

There are obvious exceptions. Perhaps your parents are separated or one has died. Maybe you live in a foster home or have adoptive parents. Whatever your particular situation, God has probably placed someone in a position of parental authority in your life. You owe him or her a sincere debt of gratitude.

If it's hard to say thanks, perhaps you have a serious communication problem. Have you thought about how little time you spend with them? I've met many teenagers who are better acquainted with friends, teachers, and schoolmates than they are with their parents. The reason is obvious. You get to know people you talk to.

Most families congregate only to eat or watch television. Mealtime is hardly an effective open forum, since in many homes it's hurry-up time. And viewing television is not conducive to getting to know each other.

What about this suggestion? Spend your next weekend with Mom and Dad—just them! Cancel your parties and plans. Leave the television and stereo off and get acquainted with the two people who love you most. As you learn more about who they really are, you will learn more about yourself—a mutual revelation that can enrich your life immeasurably.

TWENTY

MANSION OVER THE HILLTOP

Before you return this book to your parents, I want to share a
personal experience. The Lord taught me some lessons that may
save you and your parents a lot of heartache. Please read these final
two chapters carefully.

There are two things God requires of you as a child: honor and
obedience. In the Old Testament you are told in Exodus 20:12,
"Honor thy father and thy mother that thy days may be long upon
the land."

In the New Testament we read this injunction (Eph. 6:1 and Col.
3:20): "Obey your parents."

Teenager, God promises to bless your life if you do those two
things. If you do not, the consequences are dire. In fact, the apostle
Paul declares that the end times before the return of Christ will be
evidenced by a generation that is "disobedient to parents" (2 Tim.
3:2).

The opposite of obedience is rebellion. That kind of conduct,
God declares, is tantamount to practicing witchcraft (1 Sam. 15:23).
He also declares that stubbornness equates with idolatry.

These are stern warnings, especially for this generation that
considers it fashionable to defy tradition. Many parents can no
longer control their children. More than one sobbing mother has
told me she doesn't dare discipline her son for fear of physical
retaliation.

"But I wouldn't do that," you argue. "I'd never strike my parents."

Perhaps not physically. But what about the verbal and emotional abuses you have heaped upon them? Slammed doors, pouting lips, and yelled retorts are just as serious.

"You're not going to run my life," you screamed, heading up the stairs to your bedroom.

Then you put on the earphones and played your favorite rock album. The words and sounds carried you away. The message placated your injured pride.

The songs declared over and over, "Forget the hassles. Parents don't understand. Move with the music. We're taking over some-day!"

You think I'm exaggerating? Make a list of how many popular rock artists openly honor their parents. Name the songs you've heard saying your parents know best and that success depends upon how well you follow their advice. It's a pretty short list, isn't it?

Rock entertainers' crazed world of sex and drugs doesn't promote parental respect. Few superstars bother to mention their moms and dads. That's understandable. There aren't many parents willing to publicly endorse the outlandish life-styles their children have adopted. The rock scene and the world at large won't give you much incentive to obey and honor your parents. The only real encouragement you'll get is from God's Word. Before you judge your parents too harshly, remember these facts.

FACT 1: *Parents aren't perfect.*

"Big deal," you say. "I already know that."

Then why do you act as if you expected perfection from them? Parents do make mistakes and their judgment is fallible, but it's usually better than yours.

Your parents have something you can never surpass—experi-ence. When they advise or reprimand you, they have your best interests in mind. When parents do err, it's usually a mistake of the head, not the heart. They truly want what's best for you, and sometimes their perspective is difficult for you to understand.

You can probably name a dozen times when your parents made a wrong decision that affected your life, but ask yourself how many times their advice saved you from harm.

Nowhere does God command you to honor and obey your parents with qualifications. He doesn't demand your allegiance to them because they're perceptive, intelligent, well-educated, and knowl-edgeable. God only requires that you obey.

If your parents make wrong decisions governing your life, God will hold them accountable, not you. On the other hand, if you disobey even their erroneous directives, you are the one God will hold accountable. (Keep in mind we are discussing Christian homes where parents are trying to raise their children in the fear of the Lord. Disobedience might be justified in the case of a sinful parent insisting the child indulge in unlawful or immoral behavior, in which case obedience must be accorded to the higher law of God.)

FACT 2: *Parents don't always have reasons for their advice.*

"Just give me one good reason why I can't," you protest. That plea is usually followed by the proverbial "everybody's doing it," and you question your parents' wisdom in comparison to overwhelming odds in your favor.

Are you certain that everybody is doing it? Such logic is intended to intimidate parents. After all, they wouldn't want their son or daughter to be left out. It's assumed that everybody else's parents have approved, so why should yours be different?

It takes a brave Mom and Dad to stand up to that one. But they need even more courage and fortitude to withstand the wear-down process of "give me one good reason."

You don't really care why they said no, you just want them on the defensive. Instead of obediently submitting, you demand that your parents justify their decision.

You've already made up your mind they're wrong, and it's just a matter of time until you can prove it. You assume they have no right to forbid your conduct unless they can present a rational defense for their refusal. Is your reasoning valid?

Because God made your parents responsible for your behavior, he provides them with special insight to guide your life. As a result, they may sometimes express intuitive apprehensions for which they have no discernible logic.

God places something in parents' hearts that can't be explained. They may perceive inherent dangers in a course of action you'd want to pursue. Perhaps they may not adequately articulate their fears. They just feel it, and that's why they say no.

The choice is yours. You can obey their decision and honor them, even if it means denying something you want, or you can ignore them and fulfill your own desires. Rejecting their advice may cause you to miss God's richest blessings on your life.

Perhaps the following personal illustration will convey the importance of obeying parental authority:

For several years, I had wanted to move from suburban Denver,

Colorado, and relocate in a more rural, mountainous setting. I love the outdoors and have always felt cramped by the noise and bustle of city life.

After an extensive search, I found a house that seemed perfect. Located on wooded acreage not far from town, it was conveniently close, yet relatively secluded. More important, it offered the peace and quiet I yearned for. Everything was suitable but the price, which I felt was beyond my means. It had been on the market for quite awhile, and the real estate agent suggested that I at least make an offer.

I chose an amount so low he hesitated to write a contract for fear my offer would be considered unreasonable. I was more shocked than he was when the seller accepted. It was too good to be true. A financial advisor assured me the house was underpriced, and I could easily double my money in a year if I wanted to sell. I explained the purchase to my accountant. Without exception, everyone I consulted encouraged me to go through with the deal. They all felt I had come upon a once-in-a-lifetime opportunity.

Then I called my parents.

I was so excited, I couldn't wait to tell them. After some preliminary small talk, I got to the point.

"Mom and Dad, remember that beautiful house in the mountains I showed you? Well, I made them a ridiculously low offer, and they accepted. I signed the contract today. Isn't that great?"

They were silent.

Their hesitation puzzled me. I couldn't imagine their having any apprehensions. Everyone else wanted me to buy it. Surely they would agree.

Dad was the first one to speak. "Don't do it, Son," he said.

I went limp. I didn't need their consent. My mind was already made up. As a grown man, I was certainly capable of making my own decisions. I didn't ask for their opinion, but now that I had it, what was I going to do?

I did what any son would do. I protested, "Just give me one good reason!"

They offered one, but I felt it was a feeble excuse. I shot it full of holes with my "superior" logic.

"Give me another reason," I chided.

This went on for several minutes.

Mom and Dad tried to explain their feelings. Then, I exploded their arguments by the reasonableness of my decision.

Finally, I thought they were out of ammunition, and I moved in for the kill.

"Just give me one more good reason," I insisted.

"We feel this way because we've prayed about it," they answered.

There was no retort for that one!

It did propose a nagging question to my mind. Was it possible that even at my age God could speak to me through my parents? Was I still under their jurisdiction? It was too much for me to weigh in a moment's time.

"I'll have to think this over and call you back later," I said.

The next twenty-four hours were agonizing. I was torn between my own desires and an impulse to obey my parents, regardless of what I felt were their irrational conclusions.

Finally, I reached a decision.

There seemed to be no logical reason to follow my parents' advice. Their only objection was a subjective, spiritual impression. I honestly felt I could buy that house without dishonoring them or disobeying the Lord.

Then a thought came to my mind. Perhaps God wants to take that house away so later he can give me something better.

Then I thought of something else. What if I disobeyed my parents in these closing years of their lives? Could I stand by their graves knowing that when they needed me most I rejected their advice?

I called the real estate man with whom I had signed the contract. When I informed him that we wanted to terminate the deal, he was understandably upset. Then I explained.

He listened intently and responded. "I'm Jewish," he said, "and I was taught to honor my parents in the same way. I won't hold you to the contract."

He tore it up, and I felt a sense of peace. To the logical mind, my decision made no sense. But that was irrelevant. I had obeyed my parents, and the loss of my dream house was a small price to pay for honoring them.

Were my parents right? It took me three years to learn that God, indeed, had something better in store for me. If I had disobeyed him by not honoring my parents, the following chapter could not have been written.

TWENTY-ONE
SHAMEA

"That house could have been yours."

I heard the devil say it a thousand times. He wouldn't let me forget. Every time I drove into the mountains on business or pleasure, he made sure I noticed what could have been mine.

What happened to the house? I would have preferred that termites had eaten its foundation or it had burned to the ground. But nothing bad happened. Someone came along and bought it at the same price I had offered. I resented the new owners. When they plunged into remodeling, I also resented their conceiving of improvements on my dream home.

I was content that my decision had been the Lord's will, but emotionally I wanted confirmation that I had done the honorable thing. I needed to know what I knew was right. I didn't mind obeying the Lord as long as I received adequate commendation for my moral courage. And I didn't want to wait forever to get it.

As the months passed, I grew increasingly dissatisfied with my suburban home but resigned myself to the possibility of continuing to live there with barking dogs and blaring radios. Opportunity had knocked, and I had not answered. It seemed unlikely to call again.

It is easy for God's children to forget he loves us and wants us to have the desires of our hearts when we delight ourselves in him. Too often we see God as a stern judge who only deprives and disciplines us. We think self-denial and sacrifice are the only roads to happiness and forget that once we have given, he wants to give back to us in even greater measure. Instead of approaching his blessings with joy, we timidly acknowledge them with guilt.

Would you enjoy giving gifts to your children if they received them reluctantly? Christmas would be a sad time if all you heard around the tree was, "I really don't deserve this." We give because we want to delight the recipient, and so does God.

Many young people think the Lord wants to rob their adolescent years of joy and excitement. Getting rid of that Prince album or taking down that Ozzy poster is seen as a "don't." They need to see this commitment as a "do" to open God's window of blessings.

Before God can bless you, two steps are necessary. You must say no to that which comes between you and the Lord, and you must be tested to determine if you can handle God's abundance. In short, you will need to prove the principle that faithfulness in a few things will make you worthy of being "ruler" over many things.

In my life, obedience taught me the first lesson. By honoring my parents, I demonstrated that my material desires came second to doing what was right. The second test, proving my worthiness for God's blessings, lay ahead.

For several years, the Lord had been leading me into an intensive personal ministry of counseling those bound by evil forces. That exotic and eyebrow-raising term "demon possession" had become as real and familiar as any other experience in God's Word.

At times, I opened my home to such people because a brief time of counseling was not enough for them. You can't make appointments with Satan or the Holy Spirit. Freedom from spiritual enslavement often involves a prolonged struggle, which requires resisting the devil and extending love to the one he has invaded. My home was a haven for those Satan had enslaved. It was not my dream home in the mountains, but for many it was a spiritual oasis where they could drink freely of God's liberating power.

On one such occasion, I was praying with a person who had long been involved in spiritualism and the black arts. Through a series of miraculous circumstances, God's grace had reached down to pluck this one from the grip of Satan.

Months of battling the devil's kingdom had reached a climax. I was directly confronting the violent and powerful spirit that controlled this person. The demon was manifesting itself through the voice, eyes, and other neurosensory faculties of the one for whom I was interceding.

Suddenly, as I rebuked the evil spirit in the name of the Lord, the person's head turned and the demon stared at a wall shelf.

"What are you doing?" I asked.

"I am drawing strength out of that object," the voice answered.

I turned quickly to see what the spirit had so intently set its eyes upon. There, in the corner of the room, was an ebony carving I had purchased six years earlier on the island of Bali.

"Is that the only thing you draw power from?" I demanded to know.

"No," the voice answered defiantly.

I was stunned momentarily. My home was dedicated to the Lord, and I assumed all its contents belonged to him. How could sin have so effectively entered?

My home is a veritable museum, brimming with souvenirs collected from my travels to almost every part of the world. Many artifacts were purchased cheaply in their land of origin. Other objects were presents from missionaries and friends.

Among the scores of treasured mementos were eleven objects that contained symbolic and intrinsic expressions of Satan's kingdom. When the demon revealed that certain possessions were spiritual hindrances, I immediately bound the spirit by the Word of authority. Gradually, it submerged and the person came out of a trance. "Have you noticed anything in this house that affects you adversely?" I asked.

"Oh, yes," came the reply. "I've never looked to see where the vibrations were coming from, but I felt them the moment I walked in your front door."

"Well, then," I instructed, "we're going to walk through every room while you point out everything that might displease God."

How would you have responded to that request? Imagine being invited into a home for prayer and spiritual help and finding yourself convinced that certain possessions have demonic significance. I was asking a lot of this person, whose hesitancy was understandable. Nevertheless, we walked from room to room gathering demonically influenced artifacts.

I was astonished to find things that had been overlooked for years. All these gifts and purchases had been carefully selected. None were idols or fetishes. Before buying, I always asked if there were religious significance to the items. But my caution had been insufficient.

I was shocked to find that a magnificent Indonesian watercolor had a spirit's face cleverly depicted in an obscure corner. Upon closer inspection, an African oil of a tribal chieftain portrayed a meditative trance state. One by one, the objects were taken from walls and shelves.

We descended into the basement. I knew this person had never been inside my office there. As we stepped through the door, I asked, "Is there anything here that causes the spirits to react?"

The reply came without hesitation, "Over there, on the left."

I looked in vain to discover a source of satanic expression.

"It's small, whatever it is, about six inches high."

"But all I can see is a little bronze figurine of a Thai dancer I picked up in the Bangkok airport ten years ago. It's just a cheap souvenir," I argued.

"Look closer at the face."

Its face was the size of my thumbnail. Yet some craftsman had ingeniously etched a hideous spirit's face that seemed incongruous with the graceful body.

We eventually gathered from all the rooms more than three thousand dollars' worth of objects, plus an exquisitely carved wooden desk valued at four thousand dollars. Part of it was salvageable, since only the carvings on the trim were objectionable. But the other eleven objects left me no choice.

We went back to the family room and started a fire in the fireplace. One by one, we threw objects into the flames for purification and destruction. The intensity of the heat was amplified by the ninety degree weather of a hot summer day, and the room seemed transformed into hell itself. Somehow, the brilliant flames and searing heat seemed appropriate.

Before I struck the first match, I had tried to anticipate my feelings. Would some great surge of spiritual pride overwhelm me because of the enormity of my commitment? After all, how many people would be willing to destroy three thousand dollars' worth of valued treasures?

In spite of my costly decision, I felt only shame. I had innocently purchased those items. If I had dreamed they would be a source of inspiration to Satan, I'd never have brought them into my home, but such thinking could not excuse me now.

One thought was foremost in my mind. How many other times had the Holy Spirit tried to speak and warn me that some of my possessions were a hindrance to those I was trying to help?

A profound sense of unworthiness filled me. It had taken an evil spirit to make me see the spiritual obstacles in my life, when I should have been listening to the Holy Spirit.

My situation is not unique. Perhaps these specific circumstances were extraordinary, but similarities aren't rare. I've visited many homes that display occult trinkets and idolatrous artifacts—Aztec sun signs, Buddhas, astrology plaques, tiki gods, African devil masks, kachina witch doctor dolls, ankh rings, and pendants. Many people travel abroad today, and they gather mementos that symbolize Satan's kingdom, not Christ's lordship. Some who declare that Jesus is the head of their home openly exhibit things that convey Satan's seal of ownership.

Does that mean Christians should conduct a witch hunt through their homes? Should they look for demons under every bed? Is each strange or foreign object a source of invested satanic energy? Absolutely not! It would only glorify Satan to become paranoid about evil lurking in every corner.

The Christian who walks in fellowship with Christ and abides under the blood should not fear Satan or his devices. But neither should we be ignorant of them. Deuteronomy 7:26 warns us, "Neither shalt thou bring an abomination into thine house lest thou be a cursed thing like it; but thou shalt utterly detest it and thou shalt utterly abhor it; for it is a cursed thing."

Don't think that any object by itself can bring evil into your home. Ultimately, it is the attitude of the heart that gives place to Satan. But if one's life is spiritually vulnerable, it is dangerous to harbor that which is cursed. Furthermore, the injunction of Deuteronomy 7:26 applies to more than Mom and Dad's souvenirs. It can also encompass certain rock record albums.

For teenagers who are reading this book, there is one message you should get clearly. If you want God to bless you, get the cursed things out of your life.

"But it's just one poster . . . it's just one album. You don't think just one record will hurt me spiritually, do you?"

Galatians 5:9 says, "A little leaven leaventh the whole lump."

As long as you tolerate the slightest sin in your life, the devil has a toehold. In Joshua 7, we read that the sin of one man brought defeat upon Israel. Achan kept in his possession those things which God had cursed. The result was disaster and death for an entire nation.

The Enemy only needs to find one area of your life uncommitted to Christ to gain access to the whole. Maybe that poster or record isn't an avenue of evil to hinder you spiritually, but what if it is? Is it worth hanging on to if it is cursed?

You're probably still wondering what became of my dream house. Well, it's still there, as beautiful as ever. But right across the road from it stands another, more magnificent home. Nestled among tall Ponderosa pines, it's the perfect hideaway for solitude and seclusion. The natural cedar wood exterior blends quietly into the surroundings. Outside the front door, squirrels scurry, unmolested by traffic and the hazards of civilization. From the back porch, you can look across a mountain valley on a warm summer evening and watch a herd of elk grazing in the meadow.

This is a home I would treasure as a gift from God even more than the house I almost bought. And I do, because it is mine!

How did I come to build my dream home next to the house denied me because of obedience to parental authority?

Would you believe that, through a series of circumstances, the Lord showed me the exact architectural design I should choose? Could you accept the fact that after several frustrating attempts to find a contractor, the Lord led me to the right man? He had just finished building and was planning to build again the very home the Lord had shown me three months earlier in an architectural book.

If you can't believe that, then you'd be amazed to hear of a dozen other details in both the construction and planning of this home that bore the stamp of God's miraculous intervention. It's not the world's most lavish and magnificent building, and it's not a millionaire's mansion. But there is something special about this house. It's the home God wanted for me.

If you ever drive out West and stop in Denver, there's something about my house I want you to see. When you walk in the front door, you'll immediately notice a sign above the entrance. It has one word on it—SHAMEA—Hebrew for "obedience." In the corner is a Scripture reference, Isaiah 1:19:

If ye be willing and obedient,
ye shall eat the good of the land.

GLOSSARY OF ROCK PERFORMERS

Just when a parent thinks he vaguely understands the rock scene, teenagers employ their favorite tactic: "Why can't I listen to such-and-such rock group? They aren't homosexuals, they don't use drugs, and they don't sing about sex. Can I buy one of their albums?"

What can a parent do? You've probably never heard of the group in question and have no idea if it's offensive or acceptable. You may believe there's no way to stay sufficiently informed to guide your children. You don't want to be unreasonably restrictive, but neither do you want to expose your family to immorality.

The following glossary of rock music performers was compiled with this dilemma in mind. It would be impossible to include every band on the charts. Only the better-known groups with the highest record sales in recent years have been cited. Some groups that were discussed earlier in the book are not mentioned again. Others that were given cursory attention have been analyzed further in this glossary.

What if your children bring up a name not included here? The group or person may have gained public attention after this book's publication. There are thousands of singers and musicians with the potential for stardom, and including every band would be an impossible task. Today's most popular artists may be forgotten in a few months. Bands break up, performers die, and other changes occur. Indeed, many of the artists listed in this glossary are no longer recording. Elvis, to name one obvious example, died in 1977, and the Beatles have been split up for years. But they are listed here because their influence is still felt in rock circles. Be sure to take note when this glossary states that a group is no longer together. If you want to discuss rock intelligently, don't prove your ignorance by asking about Led Zeppelin's latest album; they haven't been together for years, though you do need to know about them and the influence they've had.

One of the problems in keeping up with the rock scene is that bands come and go so quickly. Another problem is that there is no hard-and-fast definition for *rock star*. Iron Maiden is definitely a rock group, but what about Genesis, Olivia Newton-John, and Paul Simon? Such performers as these are usually considered *pop* artists, and they are not dealt with in this glossary, though some have been mentioned in passing earlier in this book. I have tried here to focus on performers that are considered rock performers by most authors and fans.

Pop performers often have immoral life-styles and sing questionable lyrics, but most don't exhibit that sex-obsessed, anti-establishment attitude of typical rock performers. You may allow your children to listen to the music of Paul Simon and Kenny Loggins; you almost certainly don't want them listening to Motley Crue and Krokus, and that is why they are listed here. If your child prefers Paul Simon's creative, rhythmic *Graceland* album to the earsplitting album *Stay Hard* by Raven, consider yourself fortunate. But if you had such a child, you probably wouldn't be reading this book anyway.

This glossary may not contain all the information you need, but it provides information about major names in the rock entertainment industry. Though the group your children ask about may not be listed, the book's basic guidelines should be helpful.

Remember as you read that Jesus Christ loves the sex-obsessed rock star as much as he loves you and your child. Christ is unwilling that any should perish (2 Pet. 3:9). Approaching this glossary on that basis will help to interpret the information constructively.

The immorality of these individuals is discussed in explicit detail because their life-styles are a matter of public record. Most knowledgeable young people already know this information, but parents need to be educated to make intelligent decisions for their children.

Some may feel my analyses are slanted toward the unsavory

aspects of rock artists, neglecting positive elements in their character and music. But what is positive isn't problematic. For this reason, some popular artists such as Genesis, Lionel Ritchie, and others are not included because, for the most part, their lyrics and life-styles are not openly immoral. My emphasis here is on the artists with the most negative moral impact upon our youth.

AC/DC
Aerosmith
The Beach Boys
Beastie Boys
The Beatles**
The Bee Gees
Pat Benatar
Black Sabbath
Blue Oyster Cult
Bon Jovi
Boston
David Bowie
Eric Clapton
Alice Cooper
Culture Club
Deep Purple
Def Leppard
Ronnie James Dio
Duran Duran
Eurythmics
Foreigner
The Grateful Dead
Hall and Oates**
Billy Idol
Iron Maiden
Jefferson Airplane/Starship
Elton John

Judas Priest
KISS
Krokus
Cyndi Lauper
Led Zeppelin**
Madonna
John Cougar Mellencamp
Motley Crue
Stevie Nicks
Ted Nugent
Ozzy Osbourne
Pink Floyd**
Elvis Presley**
The Pretenders
Prince
Queen
Ratt
The Rolling Stones
Scorpions
Bruce Springsteen
Rod Stewart
Sting
Twisted Sister
Van Halen / David Lee Roth
WASP
The Who**

**indicates a group that has a disbanded or a solo artist who has died.

AC/DC

In the 1980s, five delinquents from Down Under imported to America the firebrand hard rock that had captivated Aussies. The source of their name is controversial. According to the rock periodical *Circus,* AC/DC connotes "power and sexual ambiguity."[1] Members of the band say they got the name from the handle of their sister's vacuum cleaner in Sydney, Australia.[2] Of their 8 million-copy-selling album *Back in Black, Circus* declared, "Its death-tinged title and double entendre lyrics have made AC/DC the target of attacks by religious extremists."[3]

Dirty Deeds Done Dirt Cheap, their re-released 1978 album, said it all. Their "deeds" delineated lyrics and graphics too explicit to print here. AC/DC song titles include "Big Balls," "Love at First Feel," "Let Me Put My Love into You," and "Highway to Hell." The latter was delivered with a lascivious growl by lead singer, Bon Scott. Overtly inviting Satan to claim his soul, Scott declared hell to be the "promised land" and warned that nothing would stop him from cashing in his "season ticket" for a "one-way ride."

One night Scott passed out from an alcohol/drug overdose. When they found him the next morning, Bon Scott's arrogant affront to God had been fulfilled at age thirty-three.

Lead guitarist Angus Young and the other members regrouped, found a new singer in Brian Johnson, and hit the road again declaring in their new album that they were *Back in Black.* "Hells Bells," a hit off of the new album, showed no signs of sobered repentance. Johnson seemed to be a "reincarnation" of Scott, singing about giving "black sensations" up one's spine. "If you're into evil," he challenged, you are most certainly "a friend of mine." As a clincher he pointed out that if good could be found on the left, he'd definitely be "stickin' to the right."

Defending their macabre topics and sexual bluntness, Angus Young of the band declares, "The song 'Highway to Hell' has nothing to do with devil worship. It's about a band that was on the road a lot."[4] When asked about the song "Hell Ain't a Bad Place to Be," Young said, "We're kidding around. We're saying if you've got your choice between heaven and hell, you might take hell. In heaven you have heart music, and in hell there's a good rockin' band and rockin' songs. That's what we'd choose, so hell ain't a bad place to be."[5]

Brian Johnson is more honest about the evil in their songs. Johnson declares, "I'm scared to death by the energy we put into our music. Sometimes it seems that Bon Scott's ghost is right up there with us. It's a very strange feeling."[6]

Critics have called AC/DC's hell-raising music infantile, but loyal fans (mostly male) know AC/DC's on-stage persona isn't an act. Explaining their song "The Jack" (a British term for gonorrhea), Bon Scott once told an interviewer, "We were living in this household of very friendly ladies, and everyone got the jack. So we wrote this song."[7] One prorock journal commented on Scott's death by observing, "Throughout the AC/DC catalogue there is a disturbing correlation between pleasure/sex/drunkenness and unconsciousness/death, which has now reached its tragic culmination."[8]

Their approach may seem moronic and barbaric, but there is no hype in the way the band sings and lives. *If You Want Blood (You've Got It),* an earlier album, shows AC/DC's guitarist impaled on the neck of a guitar, lying on the floor drenched in blood. This writer once asked a rock musician who covers versions of AC/DC songs to comment on the significance of this depiction. "Rock 'n' roll kills," he calmly replied with all seriousness. It did kill Bon Scott. The haunting question is, "Who's next?"

1. *Circus,* February 28, 1986, p.34.   2. *People,* January 30, 1984, p. 42.
3. *Circus,* February 28, 1986, p. 34.   4. *The Sunday Peninsula Herald,* October 13, 1985.   5. Ibid.   6. *Hit Parader,* August 1982, pp. 58-59.   7. *Circus,* January 30, 1980, p. 34.   8. Ibid., p. 35.

AEROSMITH

The soft sounds of the 1970s didn't deter this hard-driving Boston band. Their albums sold millions, and one of them, *Toys in the Attic,* was on the charts for 150 weeks. Faithful audiences of eighty thousand came to hear them churn out deadening metal sounds and profane lyrics.

The group focused on its androgynous lead singer, Steve Tyler. A pedometer clocked his stage movements during a concert for a total of four miles per performance. Tyler crooned of the cheerleader who was a "young bleeder" and the short-skirted girl with a "kitty in the middle." His fantasies were fulfilled with Cyrinda Fox, whom he married after she became pregnant with his child. When police busted fifty-two young people for drug abuse at one of its concerts, Aerosmith paid $3,650 to bail them out. Tyler boasted of his arrest for drugs while in the eleventh grade.

After its heyday in the seventies, Aerosmith conceded to clones like Motley Clue and Ratt. When Aerosmith regrouped after several years' absence from the rock scene, its ardor for evil hadn't subsided.

Joe Perry declared, "Everybody does drugs. Everyone has their
own drugs, whether it's eating [sexual expletive] or being gay. I'm
not advocating them and I don't choose to do them before I go on
stage, but when you go on the road there's nothing to do but to do
drugs and [sexual expletive]."

The band's "reunion" album was *Done with Mirrors,* which did
little to prove that the band had mellowed. *Billboard* magazine
commented of their new act, "Elaborate staging was eschewed in
favor of antic behavior and liberal use of obscenities . . . and the
one word of more than four letters Steve Tyler uttered begins with
'mother.' "[1]

1. *Billboard,* February 15, 1986, p. 47.

THE BEACH BOYS

While most sixties groups faded with the onslaught of psychedelia,
the Beach Boys survived both musical and personal changes and
managed to excite a whole new generation of rock fans to whom
they were old enough to be fathers. Their durability and close
harmonies sold 80 million records in their first fifteen years together.
While their early songs may have been innocuous tributes to high
school pursuits, their personal involvement in more serious matters
influenced many. The all-American California surfers delved into
LSD (Brian Wilson), flirtation with the Manson family (Dennis
Wilson), and Transcendental Meditation (Mike Love and Al Jardine).
The Christian teenager who nostalgically bounces to "Surfin'
U.S.A." should remember that the Beach Boys' fame prepared the
way for the Maharishi Mahesh Yogi's introduction of TM and occult
mysticism into America's mainstream.

BEASTIE BOYS

These three young men aren't musicians, and they don't sing. They
are rap artists, using the style of black groups like Run DMC and
fast-talking the American public into buying millions of records.
They started out as a hard-core punk band. Their first release,
"Cookie Puss," featured a taped conversation of the Boys harassing
female employees at an ice cream store in New York. Appropriately,
they named themselves the Beastie Boys.

The three Beasties have each adopted rap nicknames. Adam

Yauch is MCA, Michael Diamond is Mike D, and Adam Horovitz is King Adrock. Their debut album, *Licensed to Ill,* pictures on the cover a 727 jet smashed nose first into the ground. Advertisements for the album declared, "An album guaranteed to bug your parents (or someone you love)." (Columbia Records chose not to release the album under its working title, *Don't Be a Faggot.*) The album was described by *Rolling Stone* as a "nightmare of profanity, sex, and violence. If you don't see the joke in three white, relatively privileged brats affecting the manners and morals of street hoods, you miss the point—not to mention the fun."[1] The album became the fastest-selling debut album in Columbia's history, with sales surpassing 3 million at the time this book went to press.

The record industry was shocked by the Beasties' offensiveness. *Time* referred to them as "rock's degenerate darlings."[2] The boys reinforced that image by admitting their white punk, black rap, heavy metal sound was based on the "24-64" formula. Adrock explained the formula in this way: "After about 24 ounces of beer, the creativity begins. After 64 ounces, the babbling begins."[3] The group's stage props have included a towering Budweiser six-pack, a scantily clad go-go dancer in a chrome cage, and a twenty-foot hydraulic phallus that erects during the concert.

Parents weren't laughing at tunes like "Rhymin' and Stealin'," an ode to drinking and robbing. Another tune described the sadistic sexual act of penetrating a woman with a "whiffle ball bat." The song "Fight for Your Right (to Party!)" pokes fun at teachers, parents, and authority in general. The song's video shows a wild party scene. One Beastie puts an aphrodisiac into the punch, and another tries to seduce a series of girls.

In a *Spin* magazine interview, the boys claimed that their favorite book was *Extended Sexual Orgasm.* One of the Beasties said it is the "book the Beastie Boys live by . . . it talks about ways to make your girlfriend, or any other girl, have an orgasm for an hour or more. We're not talking about multiple orgasms or an orgasm that lasts an extraordinary length of time, like thirty seconds. We're talking about a new plateau beyond the wildest imagination."

Columbia Records has expressed some concern about the group's behavior. But as record sales soared, a Columbia spokesman said, "Two million records alleviates a lot of nervousness. It's good to be bad when it makes money."[4]

1. *Rolling Stone,* February 12, 1987, p. 18. 2. *Time,* February 23, 1987, p. 92.
3. Ibid. 4. *People,* March 9, 1987, p. 31.

THE BEATLES**

Why analyze a group that no longer exists? Because the Beatles
endure through their music, and, as Shakespeare put it, "The evil
that men do lives after them." What the Beatles said in the 1960s set
the tone for topics as diverse as drugs, war, parents, and respect for
authority. Their melodies melded into our consciousness. (Where
would Muzak be without "Yesterday" and "Michelle"?) The lyrics
and life-styles of the Fabulous Four sparked a revolution and altered
society's perception of public decency. The erotic escapades of John
and Yoko, the glorification of drug experimentation via "I Get High
with a Little Help from My Friends," and the Beatles' espousal of
TM affected the values of millions. John, Paul, George, and Ringo
taught us to accept pop idols as arbiters of sex, politics, and religion.
The Beatles may have been only temporarily "more popular than
Jesus," but it was long enough to alter the Western world's music
and morals.

In 1987 Beatles albums were released in a new form—compact
discs. Record stores were ecstatic over sales, and youth who were
not even alive when the Beatles landed in America in the early
sixties flocked to buy the perfectly rerecorded sounds of the band.
Along with many people of the Baby Boomer generation who still
have an undying affection for the Beatles, the youth proved that a
band's breakup doesn't necessarily mean that their records don't sell
or that their influence is gone.

THE BEE GEES

Known as the Bee Gees, Barry, Robin, and Maurice Gibb (Brothers
Gibb), achieved a domination of the pop charts not seen since the
Beatles. With the help of *Saturday Night Fever,* the movie for which
they penned most of the tunes, the Bee Gees were expected to gross
$210 million in one year. After an early string of 1960s hits, the
brothers fell into a period of drugs and division. With the help of the
disco craze and a return to concentration on falsetto harmonies, the
Bee Gees found a new following and fame. At one point, half of the
Top Ten hits belonged to them, bringing their No. 1 hit totals to the
largest of any artist or group of the 1970s.

Though their public image exuded wholesomeness, interviews on
their private lives revealed they were less than paragons of virtue.[1]
Robin confessed to a hobby of pornographic drawings. Barry

insisted that the 1979 album *Spirits Having Flown* is infiltrated with references to reincarnation, while Maurice and Robin claimed to have psychic ESP powers. Their fascination with the occult, coupled with a propensity for perverse language, made their hit "Too Much Heaven" sound like a contradiction of interests, as well as destinations.

They continue to record, working out of their Miami recording studio, but their 1981 album *Living Eyes* did not do well.

1. *Rolling Stone*, May 17, 1979.

PAT BENATAR

"Hit Me with Your Best Shot," Pat Benatar invites with sadomasochistic sauciness, hardly the challenge one expects from a diminutive, ninety-pound rock sex-kitten. Her stage presence is sassy and brazen, as she struts about in her Spandex suit. Songs like "Fire and Ice" and "Take It Any Way You Want It" enhance her image of women striking back against men rather than limping away brokenhearted. Her video for the song "Love Is a Battlefield" reinforced this aggressive image.

Whether her raunchiness is real or contrived matters little to her male audience, who find her parody of female machismo perversely alluring.

But Pat, trained as an opera singer, has expressed some misgivings about her sexy image. Concerned that her record company once produced an ad in which part of her leotard top was airbrushed away to make her appear naked, Pat commented, "If that is gonna sell records, then it's a real sorry thing."[1] Commenting on her stage persona, Pat says, "It was never my intention to be real obvious. It's OK to be sexual, sensual, whatever you want to do, but I think it should have class."[2]

She admits that drugs caused her first marriage to disintegrate and that her current offstage domestic life-style doesn't include drugs. Now that she is a mother, her image is changing. Pat says, "I can't be expected to do what my fans want. I can't keep wearing black tights for the rest of my life. I'm not the Peter Pan hooker that people may think I am from watching my videos." Her recording of the sweetly innocent "Here's My Heart" for the film *Metropolis* may be an indication that her sexy image is being abandoned.

1. *Rolling Stone*, October 16, 1980, p. 13.   2. *Hit Parader*, July 1982, p. 59.

BLACK SABBATH

Former lead singer Ozzy Osbourne has his own idea about how they got the name. He says, "We were sitting around, and this old Boris Karloff horror movie came on television. It was called 'Black Sabbath.' Everybody was talking around preaching peace and love, but we wanted to go in the opposite direction. We formed Black Sabbath to explore the darker side of everyone's personality."[1]

Their career began with publicity stunts like holding black masses before concerts (complete with a nude on an altar sprinkled with chicken blood). Their first album pictured the inverted cross of Christ. A later album, *Sabbath, Bloody Sabbath,* depicted a nude satanic ritual with the numbers 666 emblazoned across the front, associations that made the name Black Sabbath seem appropriate. Their aggressiveness, the droning lyrics, and blast-furnance bass fit their public relations image. Bumpers stickers boasted, "I'm possessed by Black Sabbath," and fan club T-shirts displayed a skull-and-crossbones with the Antichrist's designation, 666.

An album entitled *Born Again* featured a demonic baby with satanic horns, fangs, and claws on its fingers. Lyrics spoke of a "prince of evil" that fought for people's minds. An ad in *Billboard* magazine for *Born Again* featured a hexagram with black magic symbols and the byline, "Hitting below the Bible Belt."

Their album *Mob Rules,* released in late 1981, showed hooded beings with no faces holding whips in their hands. A sheet hangs in the center with the horned visage of Lucifer etched in blood.

The band has gone through several changes since lead singer Ozzy's departure. For awhile, Ian Gillan, formerly with Deep Purple, took over the job. When asked about the satanic aspects of the band, Gillan said, "I don't know if Tony and Geezer [band members] were into devil worship or not. All I know is that when we were recording the album 'Born Again,' which we did at this big castle, they would wake up at four in the afternoon. I don't know what they would do. They wouldn't start recording until late at night."[2]

Tony Iommi, lead singer for a while, commented on Black Sabbath's evil aspects by declaring, "Various things of the world beyond I've always had a deep fascination for. That's the super-natural, an area I'm very interested in. Much of Black Sabbath is a warning against black magic, against things you don't understand. If you don't understand it, don't practice it."[3] In 1986, Dave Donat became lead vocalist, following the footsteps of Ozzy, Iommi, Gillan, and Ronnie James Dio.

As their popularity grew, the band sought to shed their earlier black magic image. Still, one rock periodical says, "They demonstrate an almost hellish power over the audience."[4]

Just when rock critics thought Punk and New Wave had buried heavy metal, Black Sabbath resurrected and baptized audiences with downer-depressive sounds. Without Ozzy Osbourne, singer Ronnie James Dio maintained demonic overtones by flashing the audience an "Il Cornuto," the Sicilian sign for "the horn."[5] With his fist thrust into the air, index and pinky fingers extended, Dio's black magic devil's salute reinforced Sabbath as rock's foremost satanic group.

More unsettling was Dio's invitation that audiences mimic the sign and direct their attention to an onstage cross, timed to burst into flames.[6] Dio declared that his role as head vocalist maintained the group's sense of "mysticism and doom."[7] Sabbath tried to tone down its occult image, but diehard fans weren't disillusioned. They were described by a rock magazine as the kind who "get wasted, mindless, and let a black menacing cross wave over them for the evening."[8]

When someone stole a special guitar owned by Tony Iommi (the "axe" had thirteen crosses inlaid on the fretboard), fellow bandmember Geezer Butler put a hex on the unfortunate criminal. The guitar had been stolen before but was quickly returned by a repentant thief, who confessed that unending misery and tragedy had been his lot while he had the guitar in his hands.[9] Might the same be said for Black Sabbath fans who cherish their albums? Black Sabbath has used satanic symbols and encouraged demonic overtones in its musical formats to sell records. Sabbath's album *Heaven and Hell* could well be seen as a foreboding choice indead of a religious commentary.

1. *Hit Parader,* August 1986, p. 6.   2. *Hit Parader,* June 1985, p. 61.   3. *Washington Times,* April 16, 1986.   4. *Circus,* February 1976, p. 60.   5. *Circus,* August 26, 1980, p.22.   6. *Billboard,* November 1, 1980, p. 34.   7. *Rolling Stone,* May 15, 1980, p. 34.   8. *Circus,* March 31, 1981, p. 30.   9. *The Vancouver Sun,* August 22, 1980.

BLUE OYSTER CULT

What can you expect from a group named Blue Oyster Cult? As America's answer to Black Sabbath, their songs live up to their sinister name. A rock reviewer said, "This Long Island quintet continues to be to pop music what the Ouija board is to parlor games."[1] Describing the demonic character of this grinding, heavy metal music, lead singer Eric Bloom says, "It's got to be not oppressive, but felt!"

But their potent hard-rock sounds are the least of worries. Blue Oyster Cult lyrics describe death in its "Sunday best" and implore listeners, "Don't Turn Your Back" on "intuition" and "superstition." Their album *Fire of Unknown Origin* dispelled any doubts about the intent of their songs with titles like "Veteran of Psychic Wars" and "Vengeance (The Pact)." (The latter comes complete with a laughing voice, as an arrow is thrust through the head of a nameless person.) "Don't Fear the Reaper" counseled a teenage suicide love pact. "Tenderloin" described the gay district of San Francisco, and "E.T.I." was dedicated to the belief in extraterrestrial intelligences. In concert, their haunting lyrics are accompanied by a laser light show labeled by the Food and Drug Administration as visually dangerous to concert-goers. With their heavy metal sounds and sadistic, leather overtones, perhaps the same can be said of their music.

On "After Dark" the group proclaims devotion to the devil by addressing an unnamed essence whose voice calls from "far away." The singer responds because he has "no choice" after "terror took control." He goes on to extol the satanic virtues of darkness and concludes that this affinity has brought him "true salvation," with "power" as the ultimate "drug" he has been seeking. The final echoing scream may warm the hearts of committed Blue Oyster Cult fans, but it chills the spines of Christians who know the source of this "power."

1. *People*, September 14, 1981.

BON JOVI

The band is composed of Tico Torres on drums, Richie Sambora on guitar, David Bryan on keyboards, and Alic John-Such on bass. But it's Bon Jovi, guitar in hand and long curls flying, who attracts attention. Born Jon Bongiovi in suburban Sayerville, New Jersey, his parents encouraged an early interest in music by giving him an acoustic guitar. The first commercial success came when the album *7800 F* sold more than 500,000 copies. Later came the double-platinum album *Slippery When Wet,* which made real stars of Bon Jovi.

Recorded in Vancouver, the album credits the city with being the stripper capital of the world and inspiring the album title. Bon Jovi described one night in a stripper bar when an unclad young woman showering in a Plexiglas booth tried to get his attention by rubbing against the booth.[1] Consequently, the original cover for the album showed a dancer in a wet T-shirt. When radio stations and distributors complained, the cover was changed to a rain-slicked black surface with the title finger-scrawled across it. But the inner sleeve still had pictures of scantily clad girls washing cars.

Bon Jovi's first hit single was "You Give Love a Bad Name." According to the lyrics, the girl with the angel smile puts the man through hell. "The damage is done . . . you're to blame . . . you give love a bad name." With their libidinous attitude, Bon Jovi gives the caring love spoken of in 1 Corinthians 13 a very bad name.

1. *Circus,* November 30, 1987, p. 57.

BOSTON

For hard-rockers who lamented the popularity of disco and softer sounds, Boston was a welcome, deafening sonic relief. Led by Tom Scholz, a twenty-nine-year-old MIT graduate, Boston's first album soared from obscurity to sell 3.5 million copies. (Scholz worked in the Research and Development Division of Polaroid and has been described as an electronic genius.) Riding to success on its initial hit, "More Than a Feeling," Boston triggered enthusiastic audience response by asking for marijuana joints as a prelude to their tune "Smokin'." After an extended absence from the music scene, they returned in the mid-eighties much mellower, as their hit "Amanda" testified.

DAVID BOWIE

Newsweek called Bowie "the single most influential rock artist of the last ten years." The first pop music star to openly proclaim his homosexuality, David Bowie set the stage for other artists to come out of the closet. His exwife, Angela, was kicked out of a Connecticut college because of her lesbianism. The two met, *People* magazine reported, while involved with the same man.[1] Bowie also confessed to drug addiction, from heroin to cocaine. He admits, "Actually, I was junked out of my mind most of the time. You can do good things with drugs, but then comes the long decline."[2] Bowie said of the medium that propelled his rise to stardom, "Rock 'n' roll has always been the devil's music. It could well bring about a very evil feeling in the West."[3]

References to decadence in his songs and performances are too numerous to mention. Perhaps his own flaunting of perversion is what led Bowie to finally conclude, "I've never been in love. Love is a disease that breeds jealousy, anxiety, and brute anger."[4] Regarding Bowie's adaptation to stardom, *Newsweek* said he began his career wearing "lace boots with stacked heels, his face painted with makeup, his hair teased and dyed carrot orange." Now, according to *Newsweek,* he travels as a "matinee idol—our culture's masculine ideal writ large."[5]

When his exwife, Angela Bowie, was asked how it felt to be married to "the world's king faggot," she replied, "I think it's great. It all depends upon your knowledge of gay culture, of which I can happily say I'm a member." *Time* reported, "Thursday night was gay night. David would go to a gay club, Angie to a lesbian club, and they would bring home people they found."[6] Tony Visconti, who lived with David and Angie outside London in the late 1960s, says, "We had to lock our bedroom door because in the middle of the night these people Dave brought back home with them would come climbing into new beds looking for fresh blood."[7]

Older and wiser, Bowie now condemns the drug-oriented, morally loose environment of the rock culture. He refers to it as an influence that "hasn't done anything except produce casualties."[8] Of that comment, one news periodical declared tongue-in-cheek, "Bowie ought to know that area the way an old sea hand knows his charts. He navigated and narrowly missed cracking up."[9]

1. *People,* August 18, 1975, p. 68.   2. *Rolling Stone,* January 12, 1978, p. 13. 3. Ibid., p. 83.   4. *Newsweek,* July 18, 1983, p. 76.   5. Ibid., p. 77.   6. *Time,* July 18, 1983, p. 58.   7. Ibid.   8. Ibid., p. 57.   9. Ibid.

ERIC CLAPTON

Many acclaim Eric Clapton as the most accomplished guitarist of his generation. With groups like Cream, he established himself as one of the first true "superstar" musicians. A later descent into heroin addiction, which he treated with acupuncture, caused a period of decline. Of his bout with drugs, Clapton says, "I had my first taste and thought, 'Oh, you know, one snort can't do me any harm.' But . . . dead wrong!"[1] However, Clapton later recorded the immensely popular "Cocaine," a blatant prodrug anthem. A brief commitment to Christ, from which he later recanted, resulted in his writing "In the Presence of the Lord."

1. *Rolling Stone,* July 18, 1974, p. 74.

ALICE COOPER

Vincent Furnier, the preacher's son from Arizona, rose to fame as Alice Cooper by giving his fans exhibitions of transvestism, snakes, mutilated chickens, and mock public executions. His albums explored ever-deepening stages of perversion. *School's Out* featured its vinyl encased in disposable women's panties. *Billion Dollar Babies* pictured a baby made up with Cooper-style mascara. *Muscle of Love* extolled the pleasure of masturbation. *Welcome to My Nightmare* was staged by Alice simulating necrophiliac sex with a lifelike manne-quin. *Alice Cooper Goes to Hell* brought the rouge-rock queen to an encounter with the devil, referred to as "the greatest, number one."

In the song "Simple Disobedience," Cooper declares, "All the hungry outlaws have taken up a stance, simple disobedience." Alice goes beyond rebellion with sick sex and sadomasochism in the song "Trick Bag," singing, "Strap you down, honey, pet you nice with my velvet glove, I'm in the mood for my leather boots."

Such outrages brought Cooper immense wealth and ultimate respectability. After turning the stomachs and minds of fifteen-year-olds, he unleashed his lewd theatrics on adult Tahoe casino-goers. As he staged even more violent and shocking acts, Cooper, who once declared, "No more Mr. Nice Guy," sought refuge among Hollywood's in-crowd. He played golf with George Burns and helped rebuild the city's crumbling hillside sign.

Cooper's ambisexual horror shows finally descended into a desperate bout of alcoholism. Though he once credited his fame to possession by a seventeenth-century witch's spirit, Alice's age and physical exhaustion caught up with him. Thousands of impression-able teens idolized Alice Cooper as the epitome of rebellion, and, regrettably, many of his fans probably explored his perverted parodies.

Attempting a return to fame, Cooper recorded an album entitled

Constrictor. On the front of the record, a live boa constrictor en-twines itself around his face and neck, and part of the snake's body disappears into his mouth. One song from the album, "He's Back," was the theme for the murderous movie *Friday the 13th—Part VI*. For his promotional tour, Alice featured the usual doll decapitations and bloodbaths on stage. He added two scantily clad females, whom he attacked with whips, and a Frankenstein-like monster that came to life and was eventually slain by Alice.[1]

Though older and (supposedly) dried out, Alice Cooper has no intention of changing his style. In an interview on his 1987 tour he stated, "I want to take everyone on an emotional roller coaster. I want them to feel the madness."[2] Cooper was wearing the same leather outfit he wore a decade earlier on his Billion Dollar Babies tour, proof that perverse rockers can always find an audience.

1. *Hit Parader,* May 1987, p. 16.   2. Ibid.

CULTURE CLUB

More than a decade after David Bowie introduced drag into rock, Boy George flounced upon the scene in fancy prints and pancake makeup, declaring, "I don't believe people should be defined by their sexuality. I don't believe in male or female. I'm not particularly masculine, and I'm not particularly feminine. I don't think it matters."[1]

Going against the grain of most lead rock singers, who typically strike a macho pose, Boy George was deliberately sexless, sporting a porkpie hat and shapeless smocks. (Like Michael Jackson, also popular in the early eighties, Boy George seemed almost innocent in his lack of masculinity.) Fans mimicked his braided hair and smocks. And they were enchanted by the group's curious mixture of soul and white rhythm and blues. Such innocent (and often incom-prehensible) songs as "Karma Chameleon" and "Church of the Poison Mind" delighted audiences and record buyers.

But Boy George wasn't as innocent as he appeared. Some of the songs' lyrics smacked of homosexuality, with tunes like "I'll Tumble 4 Ya," suggesting homosexual oral sex. In this song, Boy George promised, "I'll be your baby, I'll be your score." While such songs were selling like crazy, his affair with another member of the group became well-known. And on the group's 1984 tour, Boy George announced to audiences that he would like to sleep with each member of the audience individually .

Tongue-in-cheek, Boy George spoke flippantly of his androgynous behavior. When *Rolling Stone* magazine asked if he were bisexual, he said, "Yeah, when I want sex I have to buy it."[2]

His spiritual views were described bluntly in another interview: "I don't believe in God, that there's somebody up there with a bowl of rice waiting to feed us. I believe in life after death. I think we all end up as maggots and that sort of thing. After all, we fertilize the earth."[3]

When Culture Club accepted a Grammy Award as the best new artist of 1983, George puckishly praised the American television audience for recognizing "a good drag queen when you see one."[4]

Their first album, *Kissing to Be Clever,* boasted three Top Ten hits, the first time for a British group in an American debut since the Beatles. But in 1986, after the dismal sales of the albums *Waking Up with the House on Fire* and *From Luxury to Heartache,* Boy George came out of another closet—the drug closet. He was arrested and charged with heroin possession. The parents of a young man who died of a drug overdose in his apartment filed a multimillion dollar suit. Boy George, who once said, "I don't do drugs. I never have,"[5] finally reaped the whirlwind of abuse and perversion he had sown.

1. *Rolling Stone,* February 11, 1983, pp. 43-45.   2. *Rolling Stone,* February 17, 1983, p. 43.   3. *Campus Life,* April 1984, p. 40.   4. *People,* April 23, 1984, p. 94. 5. *Rolling Stone,* June 7, 1984, p. 13.

DEEP PURPLE

Living proof that old rock stars can maintain an audience, Deep Purple, formed in Britain in 1968, has undergone numerous personnel changes but is still recording. The group's chief danger to listeners seems to lie in the occult/satanist tendencies of guitarist Ritchie Blackmore, who split for awhile to form the group Rainbow but is now back with Deep Purple. Blackmore is covered in detail in Chapter 7.

DEF LEPPARD

Entitled *Pyromania,* the album jacket featured a burning skyscraper with a gun sight centered over the most intense portion of the flame. If you think an album portraying arson isn't humorous, neither are Def Leppard's other antics. Their tune "Photograph," a song about sexual frustration, speaks of caged women flashing switchblades. Joe Elliot of the band says, "People always ask me how we got the name of Def Leppard. Actually, it came from a poster depicting a rather strange-looking jungle cat with a hearing horn in his ear."[1] None of the members claim to use drugs, but Elliot says, "We used to drink a lot. Now we drink more."[2]

Billboard magazine said of their fans, "They are the classic example of stand-on-the-chairs, wave-your-fist, scream-yourself-hoarse audience. They call this head-banger music, not so much for its sheer volume but because it's about as subtle as being hit between the eyes with a two-by-four."[3] El Paso, Texas, boycotted their albums after they referred to the town as "a place with all the greasy Mexicans."[4] Sexual images are also included in their music, such as "Rock-Rock ('Til You Drop)" declaring, "Come along with me, your mama don't mind what your mama don't see."

But most disturbing is their so-called arson-oriented rock and the irresponsibility of choosing such reprehensible themes. What can be expected when Joe Elliot says, "When we recorded this album, we tried to get ourselves as drunk as possible."[5]

1. *Hit Parader,* August 1983, p. 64.   2. *Rolling Stone,* July 7, 1983, p. 43.
3. *Billboard,* September 24, 1983, p. 38.   4. *People,* November 18, 1983, p. 188.
5. *Hit Parader,* November 1982, p. 61.

RONNIE JAMES DIO

His album *Holy Diver* pictures a cleric wrapped in chains being thrust into the sea. Standing above him as tormentor is a symbol of Satan, a horned figure with his index and little fingers extended in the satanic salute. Dressing in black and admitting to astro-projecting on stage, Dio has been accused of satanic collusion. Dio says, "Just because I choose to explore topics that touch on mythology, I'm labeled a devil worshiper. At least I understand something about the occult, which is more than I can say about certain bands that use pentagrams and upside-down crosses as their emblems."

But Dio's lyrics aren't as convincing as his protestation. In the song "The Last in Line," he talks about going off to see a witch, declaring, "We may never come home." He then says we are all born "upon the cross" to learn if we are "evil or divine." The stage for his "Sacred Heart" album tour featured a leering, red-eyed creature symbolizing Satan. Dio declares, "There's so many negative things associated with heavy metal these days—blood, guts, and a mentality that often seems nonexistent—our music is escape from reality."[1] But in his song "The King of Rock 'n' Roll," he sings of the monarch. "He'll scratch your soul, he's the king of rock 'n' roll."

Adding to the ambivalence, Dio says, "Jimmy Page [former lead guitarist for Led Zeppelin] is heavily into black magic. I've just been involved in white magic, which is for good and not for bad, by that I mean like having contact with the spirit world via seances."[2]

1. *Hit Parader*, February 1986, p. 9.   2. *Birmingham News*, September 26, 1985, p. 10D.

DURAN DURAN

This British group calls its music pure, escapist entertainment. You can dance to it, and you don't have to worry about lyrics that dwell on the world's problems. They are good-looking and adored as sex objects by millions of young fans. Sex, in fact, is a major theme of their music, so it's not surprising their fans often send them X-rated photos. The name of the group came from a character in the movie *Barbarella,* a criminal who makes an orgasmatron, a machine that drives girls into erotic frenzies. Duran Duran in *Barbarella* used his machine to exhaust women, then take advantage of their weakened condition.

Their video, *Girls on Film,* received special editing for MTV because network producers thought it was too sexually explicit. John Taylor of the group contributed a song to the soundtrack of the pornographic film *Nine and a Half Weeks,* which symbolized sadomasochistic relationships. Lead singer Simon LeBon, who almost died when his yacht overturned, also had problems with drugs. He says, "The worst thing they do is diminish your ability to savor sex. The thing I like is that time when you almost touch souls. I just think sex feels so good."[1]

All members of the band wear heavy makeup. Regarding their appearance, Nick Rhodes of the group says, "We wear makeup for fun. We're about entertainment, pursuing private enterprise, and people doing things for themselves."[2]

1. *People*, July 22, 1985, p. 75.   2. *USA Today*, February 13, 1984, p. 5D.

EURYTHMICS

What Boy George did for male androgyny, Annie Lennox of the Eurythmics accomplished for female gender-benders. Throughout her early career she emphasized sexual ambiguity. Great Britain banned the song "Sweet Dreams Are Made of This" because of its transvestite overtones. At a Grammy Awards show she performed dressed as Elvis Presley. The video for "Who's That Girl?" ends with Annie as both a man and a woman kissing herself. Annie says, "There have always been gender benders, and there always will be. I don't know if people think I'm gay or what. I never felt cross-dressing took away my feminity. If I were forced to wear a miniskirt, I'd have to see a psychiatrist."[1]

In the late 1980s Annie adopted a new image, seen in sexy publicity shots in which she wore a black lace bra. Her once orange hair was dyed platinum. Annie explained, "I feel like we're at the stage now where we can evoke sensuality without feeling it's being manipulated by anybody other than ourselves."[2]

This British duo exemplifies the slick, synthesized pop-rock sound that appeals to both teens and those well past their teens. Annie Lennox and Dave Stewart have produced such repetitive but ingratiating hits as "Sweet Dreams Are Made of This," "Love Is a Stranger in an Open Car," "Here Comes the Rain Again," and "Thorn in My Side." Annie, a former model, has a beautiful face, but her shortly cropped hair (almost a crew cut), men's ties, and stage manner exuded a sadomasochistic air. This became obvious in the video for "Thorn in My Side," a leather-clad illustration for a song that is almost a hymn to women giving the brush-off to men. Some of the lyrics to "Sweet Dreams" also suggest sadomasochism: "Some of them want to abuse you, some of them want to be abused." While the Eurythmics' songs are tame compared to many of the groups listed in this glossary, their apparent flirtation with sadomasochism is something worth considering. One also wonders what effect such macho-mannered women as Annie Lennox have on the feminity of female fans.

One also wonders about songs like "Missionary Man," in which Annie sings about her mother's warning not to mess with a mission-ary man because "he's got God on his side" and also has "the saints and apostles backing up from behind." In spite of the Eurythmics' sophisticated music, the sexual ambiguity and songs like "Mission-ary Man" make them a highly questionable group to listen to and support.

1. *Rolling Stone,* no date.   2. *USA Today,* August 13, 1986, p. 4D.

FOREIGNER

The touching "I Want to Know What Love Is" was a Number 1 hit by this group, but it is not typical of their work. The same group that moved 1985 listeners with their song about the search for true love has also had such hits as "Dirty White Boy," "Waiting for a Girl Like You," and "Cold as Ice." "Hotblooded," a major hit in 1978, had the singer asking a young girl, "Come on, baby, can you do more than dance?" and trying to coax her away from her boyfriend for a quick sexual encounter. "Urgent" is self-explanatory; it is an expression of desire for a brief sexual fling, with no commitment and no real interest in love. Listeners who enjoyed "I Want to Know What Love Is" need to know that Foreigner, like so many rock bands, sings more about salacious sex than about genuine love.

THE GRATEFUL DEAD

The Grateful Dead is a Frisco band that best symbolizes the era of flower power. Lead guitarist Jerry Garcia declared, "Acid rock is music you listen to when you are high on acid."[1] Their concerts are frequented by faithful legions of "dead-heads," whose attendance is marked by heavy drug usage. Age and affluence have mellowed the group little, as evidenced by Garcia's conviction for possession of LSD, pot, and cocaine. Ron "Pigpen" McKernan, considered the band's most creative musician, died from the self-destructive ingestion of alcohol and drugs. The message seems lost on those remaining. "Our lives are controlled by music," Garcia concedes.[2]

1. *Rolling Stone*, February 3, 1972, p. 30.   2. *People*, July 12, 1976, p. 50.

HALL AND OATES**

The now disbanded duo of Daryl Hall and John Oates was one of the more successful groups in a musical idiom emphasizing solo artists. As the biggest selling musical duo in rock history, Hall and Oates mimicked black sounds with the fervor of white soul. Sex was a frequent subject, as in their tune "Maneater," describing an adulteress on the prowl for money. The song says, "If you're in it for love, you ain't gonna get too far." Of the blunt language in their lyrics, Hall said, "I wish you were allowed to use more raw language. You should be allowed to say F--- in a rock 'n' roll song without being banned."[1] However, "I Can't Go for That" was a lyrical refusal to participate in sadomasochism, and "Family Man" was about a married man turning down a proposal from a woman. Still, the overall emphasis of the songs is on sex, though Hall and Oates had enough business savvy to keep things just clean enough to appeal to a wide audience.

Hall also confesses an occult background, admitting his great-grandfather was a warlock.[2] Of such inclinations, he declares, "I believe in the ability to change reality through will, and that is the definition of magic. I feel I've done that."[3] Of their sexually attractive image, Oates says, "Sometimes you can cut the energy in the room with a knife—all those teenage girls there sort of vibrating. I can't follow up on it. It would be interesting if I could. They want what they think is my body. It's fun for them to fantasize."[4]

1. *Musician,* February 1983, p. 50.   2. *Rolling Stone,* January 17, 1985, p. 22.
3. Ibid.   4. *People,* April 15, 1985, p. 50.

BILLY IDOL

His real name is William Broad, the son of a traveling salesman. Idol was originally a punk rocker with a group called Generation X. He assumed the name Billy Idol because he believed, "I can be an idol just by calling myself one." In the video for his song "White Wedding," he jams a ring on the bride's finger, causing it to bleed. In "Dancing with Myself," he shows a woman hanging in chains. Tunes like "Rebel Yell" speak of his lover in the midnight hour crying, "more, more, more." The tune "Flesh for Fantasy" describes Billy making love "navel to navel" to a woman who can "see and feel my sex attack."

"Rebellion and sexuality are the real bookends of rock 'n' roll. I'm glad there's someone around like me who says what he thinks," Idol declares.[1] Part of his appeal is his sexually threatening image— black leather pants, tattered T-shirts, spiked wristbands, and a perpetual sneer. When he performs, he strokes his body and writhes in an X-rated manner. Of drugs, he declares, "Drugs don't really alter your perception or anything that much. I mean they do, but I think if you feel pretty much in control of who you are, then drugs aren't really a problem."[2]

1. *USA Today,* August 22, 1984, p. 1D.   2. *Song Hits,* May 1984, p. 15.

IRON MAIDEN

In the days of Fats Domino and Chuck Berry, who would have dreamed that a rock group would record an album of praise to the Antichrist? *The Number of the Beast,* released by the group Iron Maiden, was such an album, featuring lines like "the number of the beast, the one for you and me." The official mascot for Iron Maiden is Eddie, a metal skeleton symbolizing death. Eddie was pictured on the front of *The Number of the Beast,* along with Satan, luring souls into the fires of hell. The album begins with a paraphrase of Revelation 13:18. The singer concludes the song by personifying the beast of Revelation, saying, "I now possess your body, and I'll let you burn." Seven of eight songs in the album pertain to death and assorted evils. The one exception is "22 Acadia Avenue," a tune about a prostitute.

When bassist Steve Harris of the band was confronted about charges of satanism, he said, "It's actually an anti-Satan song. Those who say it is should f--- themselves."[1] Harris does admit that during recording of the album there were mysterious power failures, instances of amplifiers blowing up, and radio interference. The most incredible incident was after the producer was involved in a car accident and his bill came to exactly 666 British pounds.

Exdrummer Clive Burr said, "We really don't believe in black magic. We're just interested in it."[2] Bruce Dickinson of the band says, "We're about as anti-Satan as a band can get."[3] But the touring stage for their album *Power Slave* featured a pyramid with the eye of the Egyptian god, Horus. Dickinson admits the tune "Peace of Mind" refers to Tarot card symbols.

Of the Bible, Dickinson declares, "The Bible is actually quite a happening book, as a book of philosophy or whichever way you want to look at it. Of course, there's quite a few other happening books, like the Koran, all equally right in their own ways."[4] Dickinson does admit that much of what he writes and sings is based on mythology and Egyptian black magic. He claims to have a copy of the Egyptian Book of the Dead at home and finds it "quite fascinating reading."[5]

Why does Iron Maiden have on stage replicas of the Egyptian gods Isis and her mate Osiris, god of the dead? Dickinson says, "The Egyptian idea came to me because of my interest in religion and magic and all that weird sort of stuff."[6]

Their 1985 album *Live after Death* pictures their skeletal mascot

Eddie rising out of the grave. Nearby is a tombstone quoting the words of H. P. Lovecraft: "That is not dead which can eternal lie, but with strange eons even death may die." Their futuristic album called *Somewhere in Time* features Eddie as a bionic death symbol marching down the streets of a *Blade Runner* city, ray gun in hand.

The words to "Heaven Can Wait" are of little comfort to those hoping the band's satanic imagery will subside. Written by Harris, the song speaks of "the angel of death," who's coming after his soul. The words declare, "Heaven can wait, I have a lust for the earth below." Speaking nonbiblically of eternity, Harris declares, "I'm not sure what I believe, although I do believe there are things out there that are unexplainable. The more mysterious the topic is, whether it's the occult or science fiction, the more fun it is to write about."[7]

1. *Circus,* July 31, 1983, pp. 39-42.   2. *The Calgary Sun,* June 27, 1982, p. 42.
3. *Hit Parader,* June 1984, p. 4.   4. *Circus,* February 28, 1985, p. 90.   5. *Hit Parader,* January 1985, p. 19.   6. *Hit Parader,* April 1985, p. 4.   7. *Circus,* January 31, 1983, pp. 28, 39-42.

JEFFERSON AIRPLANE/STARSHIP

Grace Slick's shrill voice and the flower power of the Haight Asbury era gave birth to this early acid rock San Francisco band. They sang the glories of drugs ("White Rabbit") and violent revolution ("Volunteers"), and they lived what they sang. Members of the band were arrested repeatedly for drug possession, causing lead guitarist Paul Kantner to comment, "The group paid for it [the drugs]. It was a business expense."[1] Grace Slick bore an illegitimate child and disdained marriage by saying, "A lot of our generation is lazy. They'd rather sit around and smoke dope than go down to the courthouse and fill out a lot of papers."[2] Blasphemy was their bag, too, as evidenced in their album *Long John Silver,* describing Jesus as a bastard who had an affair with Mary Magdalene.

Over the years, the group's name changed from Jefferson Airplane to Jefferson Starship, then simply Starship. Their interest moved from drugs to mysticism. They retained an acupuncturist to relieve tension, explored Oriental philosophy, and sang of UFOs ("Song to the Sun"). Guitarist Craig Chaquico observed, "Rock concerts are the churches of today. Music puts them on a spiritual plane. All music is God."[3]

Motherhood did slow Slick down somewhat. "It's hard to keep an eye on the kid while you're hallucinating," she admitted.[4] Her ultimate nemesis was alcohol. Few other rock bands reflected so well the counterculture from early days of hippiedom in the 1960s to the narcissistic hedonism of the 1970s.

1. *Rolling Stone,* September 30, 1971, p. 30.   2. *Newsweek,* March 16, 1971.
3. *Bay Area Music Magazine,* February 1, 1977.   4. *People,* August 28, 1978, p. 72.

ELTON JOHN

The piano's current popularity as a rock instrument reflects the influence and talent of one man: Elton John. Noted for his musical genius and clever melodies, John has sung of topics as diverse as lesbianism ("All the Young Girls Love Alice") and glue sniffing ("The Bitch Is Back"). His success has supported outlandish fetishes, such as feathered boas and two hundred pairs of glasses worth $40,000. One set has eighty-seven light bulbs that spell out his name. His father quotes him as saying, "It's all a big con. But as long as the public laps it up, I'm quite happy to go on giving it to them."[1]

While John's brilliance on the piano commands respect, his moral views are less admirable. He admits being both suicidal and bisexual. He told *Rolling Stone,* "There's nothing wrong with going to bed with somebody of your own sex. I just think people should be very free with sex—they should draw the line at goats."[2]

In February 1984 he married a twenty-eight-year-old sound engineer. (The marriage eventually failed.) His wife declared, "I've heard all sorts of stories about Elton and that he's supposed to be bisexual, but that doesn't worry me."[3] The press described Bob Halley, John's personal assistant and live-in companion for eight years, as "mute with shock." Regarding his homosexuality, Elton John told a rock periodical, "I think it hurt my record sales because it's not everybody's cup of tea. I just had to get it off my chest. I expected to offend quite a few people, but I'd rather be honest than live my life as a lie. I don't flaunt it, but I thought I could help other people like that."[4]

Elton John's 1986 hit "Nikita" caused some controversy because Nikita is almost always a man's name in Russia. The song's video showed Nikita as a woman, though her clothing and hair looked almost androgynous. With this song and many others, John proved himself a talented musician and composer—and a sexual revolutionary that Christians probably have no business supporting.

1. *Rolling Stone*, July 15, 1976, p. 30.   2. *Rolling Stone*, October 17, 1976, p. 17.
3. *Newsweek*, February 27, 1984, p. 51.   4. *Hit Parader*, September 1982, p. 25.

JUDAS PRIEST

With stage props ranging from smoke bombs to bullwhips, the bellicose, leather-clad image of Judas Priest fits its heavy-metal, earsplitting music. Rob Halford dropped some of his former stage imagery, including the motorcycle and whip. Still, violence accompanies the group wherever it goes. During a 1984 concert, fans caused considerable damage to Madison Square Garden. A reviewer declared, "The band definitely seemed amused."[1] Halford admits, "I like to think of what we do as controlled decadence. We want to stress the violence and volume, but we don't want that to be viewed as a negative element. Rock 'n' roll's the last safe outlet for hostility and tension."[2]

The sadomasochistic images continue, however. In one picture, Rob Halford appears on a motorcycle with a scantily clad girl in leather riding behind him. She wears a studded collar with an attached chain that Halford holds in his hand. Glen Tipton of the group says, "In actual fact, our image off stage isn't too dissimilar from our image on stage. We don't dress drastically different. We don't live in two different worlds."[3] Halford admits, "Sure, there may be a few unsavory things in our music, a bit of tension and hostility, but that's what the world is about these days."[4]

In response to efforts to censor songs like "Turbo Lover," the band dedicated a tune entitled "Parental Guidance." Glen Tipton says, "This tells the parents of the world to leave their kids alone. . . . We've had enough of groups of mothers telling their kids what they should or should not listen to."[5]

Critics won't be mollified with tunes like "Devil's Child" from the album *Screaming for Vengeance*. The singer describes his lover with her claws stuck into him and says, "I believe you're the devil's child." He goes on to tell how she cuts his flesh and drinks his blood. The tune "Eat Me Alive" describes oral sex so vividly the lyrics are unrepeatable. If that isn't shocking enough, K. K. Downing of the band says of their latest album, "If this album goes ignored, then watch out 'cause the next album is going to make 'em really want to vomit. We'll put together the most diabolical witch-hunting album you've ever heard."[6]

Underscoring the point, Rob Halford adds, "I know for a fact that rock's got all the elements of rebellion against your mom and dad. You want to stay up late, want to party all night long, you don't want to do your homework."[7]

Dressed in chains and studs, singer Rob Halford has been known to drop his leather drawers in midconcert. "If you're not the type of person this music can reach, then there's nothing more you can do about it. It's just a whole experience of something that happens inside of you."[9] When asked if he was personally involved in the S & M (sadomasochism) love-torture techniques parodied in his performances, Halford replied, "To a certain extent. Sexually, I have always been to the fullest extent of the experience that S & M has to offer. It's nice to experiment by yourself and get off on whatever you get off on."[10] A rock magazine ad promoting one of their albums may have said it best: "Judas Priest has sin for sale."

1. *Billboard,* July 7, 1984, p. 6.   2. *Hit Parader,* Fall 1983, p. 58.   3. *Circus,* July 31, 1982, p. 52.   4. *Hit Parader,* June 1982, p. 5.   5. *Hit Parader,* May 1981, p. 69.   6. *Circus,* August 31, 1986, p. 52.   7. *Hit Parader,* February 1983, p. 59. 8. *Billboard,* July 5, 1980, p. 28.   9. *Circus,* July 22, 1980, p. 30.   10. *Rolling Stone,* September 15, 1980, p. 14.

KISS

With Kabuki-whitened faces, they appeared on stage puking blood, declaring, "God of rock 'n' roll, we'll steal your virgin soul." Producer Bob Ezrin described KISS as "symbols of unfettered evil and sensuality."[1] Their leather/gay costuming and flair for stage violence earned the group a fanatical following, referred to as their "army." Rock magazines called them "fire-breathing demons from rock 'n' roll hell." Gene Simmons became known for his ability to lasciviously extend his tongue. On the liner notes for one album jacket, Simmons described his love techniques of "deliciously painful things that make you writhe and groan in ecstasy."[2] The album *Love Gun* contained a song dedicated to "Plaster Casters," rock music groupies who make plaster of paris replicas of famous rock stars' genitals.

In "Heaven's on Fire," Gene Simmons and company equate lust with eternal bliss as he describes his lover's heavy breathing, declaring, "Heaven's on fire." Simmons says, "Marriage is not for me. I think it's natural for man to be promiscuous, and I think any muscle you don't exercise becomes dormant."[3] "We've always been committed to warping those little minds out there who get drivel on TV, like 'Father Knows Best,' and think that's what home life is all about."[4]

Not satisfied with their erotic image, band members evoked more satanic overtones. Former band member Peter Criss boldly declared, "I find myself evil. I believe in the devil as much as God. You can use either one to get things done."[5] Gene Simmons once confessed an interest in cannibalism and said, "If God is hot stuff, why is he afraid to have other gods before him? I've always wanted to be God."[6]

"We're the cultural heroes of our day,"[7] Gene Simmons declared. Their paeans to pagan pubescence have astonished and revolted audiences all over the world. ("Cycles and whips, just all the things little girls dream about," Simmons boasted of their sadomasochistic images.)[8]

Marvel Comics produced a special edition dedicated to KISS. Blood samples were taken from the group and smeared on the plates so they could literally say the comic was printed in the band's blood. Marvel editor Steve Gerber deliberately aimed the magazine at eight- and nine-year-olds, stating that the decadence of KISS would enhance sales because the band appeals to the "baser qualities of human nature." Gerber adds, "At first, the parents' reaction will be total revulsion. Then they'll just shake their heads in dismay and go back to watching TV."[9]

Marvel's success blossomed into a small industry of KISS paraphernalia, including jeans, dolls, Halloween costumes, eye shadow, shampoo, soap, cologne, necklaces, hats, and belt buckles. A television special featured the group exhibiting psychic powers.

Whether their demented demeanor evokes images of sensuality (Simmons claims to have slept with a thousand women)[10] or violence, their stage antics have been emulated by millions of teens. Several who copied Simmons' fire-breathing exhibition suffered serious burns. One young fan killed a classmate who quarreled with him over KISS. Steve Glantz, a Detroit rock promoter, said of them, "It's almost like Hitler-rock because that audience—because of their beat, they're mesmerized by the music. They have that audience hypnotized. They could say, 'We're going out there and lift up this building,' and they'd just lift it up. That's the kind of control they have."[11]

With such control over audiences, KISS has had little respect for parents or anyone else concerned with morals. Gene Simmons stated, "If rock 'n' roll is the wheat field, then the Moral Majority is the fertilizer."[12] Simmons isn't likely to change soon, considering his attitudes toward public decency. Of his performances he says, "The stage is the place where everything goes. It's the legal zone for flashers. If it wasn't for that freedom, I'd be standing on street corners flashing old women and little girls—especially little girls. Nothing is sacred in rock 'n' roll. There's nothing that can't be done or shouldn't be done. The only limit is your imagination."[13]

After marketing their image in movies, comic books, and concerts, KISS released its own full-length video, *KISS Xposed*. An advertisement declared, "Warning: Disgusting, Titillating!!! Rare and uncensored photos of Gene Simmons and groupies in action . . . repeatedly." Like other groups that have enjoyed the rock video phenomenon, KISS is now able to bring its disgusting sensuality right into the living room.

KISS's popularity has waned in the last few years. The made-up faces and bizarre stage show had a fascination for young fans, but such acts wear thin. The group, which has undergone several personnel changes, has removed its makeup but has not maintained its large audiences. Record sales have tapered off. But no worry— KISS has already sold $60 million worth and amassed an estimated value that put them ahead of fifteen hundred corporations on the New York Stock Exchange, proof that evil and sensuality do sell and that the youth of America are willing to support raunchiness.

1. *Rolling Stone*, March 25, 1976, p. 9.   2. Ibid., p. 20.   3. *US*, January 14, 1985, p. 31.   4. Ibid., p. 30.   5. *Rolling Stone*, April 7, 1977, p. 49.   6. *Circus*, September 13, 1976, p. 42.   7. *People*, August 18, 1980, p. 100.   8. *Rock*, November 1976, p. 42.   9. *Rocky Mountain News*, April 26, 1977.   10. *People*, May 22, 1978, p. 124.   11. *Circus*, April 8, 1976, p. 27.   12. *Circus*, February 28, 1986, p. 68.   13. *Hit Parader*, June 1986, p. 13.

KROKUS

Krokus is a Swiss heavy metal band whose main interest seems to be American women's sexuality. Mark Storace of the group says, "Girls in your country have the right idea when it comes to dealing with musicians. They just want to have a good time and not worry about lasting relationships."[1] In their song, "Long Stick Goes Boom," the singer says of his genitals, "Let's do it right on the spot."

Their album entitled *One Vice at a Time* features an ad showing a number of vices listed, including depravity, lechery, sadism, voyeurism, fetishism, blasphemy, satanism, self-abuse, drunkenness, and misogyny. The ad said, "If rock 'n' roll is the ultimate vice, Krokus are prime offenders. Their latest example of excessive misconduct contains the most malicious, hard rock havoc."

Storace says, "When we're on the road, having sex is one of the things that keeps us going."[2] Storace adds, "Rock 'n' roll has always been a very sexual form, and Krokus, after all, is a rock 'n' roll band."[3]

1. *Hit Parader,* July 1982, p. 41.   2. *Hit Parader,* February 1985, p. 57.   3. *Hit Parader,* May 1986, p. 55.

CYNDI LAUPER

She has been characterized as a "New Wave Betty Boop with the heart of Janis Joplin, the lungs of a screaming punk, and the unquenching spirit of a never-say-die feminist."[1]

Diminutive Cyndi Lauper (5'3" and 108 pounds) was a self-described destructive teenager who experimented with alcohol and drugs. She ran away from home at seventeen and dropped out of school. (Her parents had divorced when she was five, leaving Cyndi's mother to support three children.) Cyndi started performing at Long Island nightclubs when she was twenty-one.

Her first album, *She's So Unusual,* beat the record set by the Beatles in 1963 for the most Top Ten singles from a debut album. It sold almost 7 million copies worldwide. Her continuing success with the album *True Colors* was partially due to her shrewd business judgment. Though some critics consider her a funny-looking girl with a funny-sounding voice, industry experts say she sticks her nose into every aspect of marketing her product. She once scoured typography books to find the right typeface for an album cover. *True Colors* took fourteen weeks to record.

Cyndi Lauper does not look like a professional businesswoman on stage. She wears clashing clothes, oversized plastic and metal trinkets, and bizarre eye makeup. Her weird hairstyles and clothing and her associations with the world of pro wrestling have led to her being nicknamed the "clown princess of rock," yet feminists adore her. Many see her as an example of free-spirited independence and feminine assertiveness, typified by such hits as "Girls Just Want to Have Fun," "Time after Time," and "All through the Night." The song "She-Bop" was almost an ode to masturbation, with Cyndi singing "I can't stop messin' with the danger zone." Christians may find Cyndi easier to take than the blatantly sexual Madonna, but Cyndi's songs have questionable lyrics, and her long-term live-in arrangement with her manager is hardly a good moral example for teens to follow.

1. *Newsweek,* March 4, 1985.

LED ZEPPELIN**

As rock entered its third decade and matured as a musical force, one band continued to top the charts and set stadium attendance records with hard-driving sounds. Led Zeppelin kept its core of raw rock, though they turned pensive occasionally with tunes like "Stairway to Heaven," a classic that was once voted the most popular tune in rock history. Their lyrics were both visionary and sexual, from "Whole Lotta Love," with unrepeatable references, to "Black Dog," which describes his lover's "honey drip." Lead guitarist Jimmy Page explained, "Rock 'n' roll is [sexual expletive]-you music."[1]

Led Zeppelin was known as much for its swinging concert tours as its music. Transported across the country in a $2,500-per-hour chartered jet complete with sauna, library, art gallery, videotape monitors, and a gourmet food gallery, the band earned a reputation for outlandish antics. In one Hollywood hotel they destroyed paintings, submerged four stereos in bathtubs, and held motorcycle races in the hallways. One rock magazine wrote about a groupie (rock prostitute) they doused with a bucket of urine and another girl who was tied to a bed with fresh fish jammed into her orifices.[2]

The group's preoccupation with sexual zaniness was less frightening than their flirtation with the occult. Lead singer Robert Plant admitted to a fascination with black magic but could hardly hold a candle to the occult interests of guitarist Jimmy Page. He owned the demon-possessed home of the late satanist, Aleister Crowley, and ran his own occult bookshop because "there was not one good collection of books on the occult in London, and I was tired of having to go all different places to get the books I wanted."[3]

To answer accusations that he is a practicing witch, Page answered unconvincingly, "I do not worship the devil. But magic does intrigue me."[4]

Zeppelin's album *Presence* displayed an oddly shaped object that Page said symbolizes the force that enabled the group to so profoundly affect audiences, a power that is referred to as a "presence." Could Led Zeppelin's enduring popularity be attributable to more than the mind-boggling heavy metal sounds that screamed from its amps?

Led Zeppelin expired in the 1980s following a series of tragedies. Lead singer Robert Plant was seriously injured in an automobile crash, Plant's son died from an unknown illness, a Zeppelin roadie also died mysteriously, and drummer John "Bonzo" Bonham was found dead on September 24, 1980. Bonham's death was officially attributed to the ingestion of "forty measures" of vodka. Traces of Motival, a drug used to curb anxiety, were also found in his blood.[5]

Bonham died in Jimmy Page's home, fueling rumors about Page's fascination with black magic. John had once declared, "I'd like to play for another twenty years. . . . I just can't see it happening . . . it's a foreboding—vultures."[6]

Most observers attributed the band's breakup to Page's satanic obsession and his veneration for occultist Crowley, whom he called "an unrecognized genius of twentieth-century thinking."[7] Bonham was known as rock 'n' roll's "bad guy" because of his reputation for destroying hotel rooms. Perhaps Bonham, known to associates as "the Beast," met his match that September evening in Crowley's former estate (Page's home). The residence is said to be haunted by a death curse, and it was Crowley who officially renamed himself "The Beast—666."

Though the group is disbanded, their records continue to sell, and many are considered rock classics. "Stairway to Heaven," heavily laden with occult overtones, is consistently voted the most popular rock song of all time. Through this song and others the group's satanic and sexual influence is still felt.

1. *Circus,* June 23, 1977, p. 35.   2. *Circus,* October 1973, p. 69.   3. *Hit Parader,* July 1975, p. 64.   4. Ibid.   5. *Rolling Stone,* November 13, 1980, p. 22. 6. *Circus,* November 30, 1980, p. 20.   7. Ibid.

MADONNA

Born the third child of eight in an Italian Catholic family, Madonna Louise Veronica Ciccone became to the 1980s what Marilyn Monroe was to the 1950s. She said of herself, "I've been called a tramp, a harlot, a slut, and the kind of girl that always ends up in the back seat of a car."[1]

Nude photos appeared in *Penthouse* magazine, and she once starred in an underground pornographic film. When an English rock magazine inquired if it was difficult to lose her virginity, Madonna replied, "No. I thought of it as a career move."[2] Explaining why she had posed nude earlier in her career, she said, "You get paid $10 an hour versus $1.50 at Burger King. I kept saying it's for art."[3]

The lyrics to her hit "Like a Virgin" described her as being "shiny and new." Her video shows something else as she rides on a gondola pursued by a lion. *Rolling Stone* said of her, "Like Prince, she recognized the virtue of a one-word name and demonstrated the truth of an old adage—sex sells. She has played America's public morals like a virtuoso, building her starlet to mega-slut to bad girl with a heart of gold to new honest woman."[4] During the Live Aid concert, she referred to her earlier undraped days, saying, "I ain't taking s--- off today."

No female artist before her had ever whipped up such an erotic frenzy, dancing like Elvis Presley and looking like a younger, more voluptuous Mae West. Young women idolized her. One female fan said, "Madonna's living out our fantasies. She's able to do something our parents would never let us get away with."[5]

Madonna wears a crucifix around her neck, see-through blouses, and fingerless gloves. She admitted the crucifix was because of her affinity for "a sexy man on a cross." But religious assertions aside, songs like "Burning Up" describe her on her knees willing to do anything as she says, "I have no shame." With her pouty, sex-kitten put-on, fans expected her fame to be short-lived, but a string of Top Ten hits gave Madonna hope for the future and fuel for her goal. In her own words, "I was born to flirt."[6] Admitting the advantages of her sexy image, Madonna stated, "I couldn't be a success without also being a sex symbol. I think people want to see me as a little tart bimbo who sells records because I'm cute.[7]

1. *People,* March 11, 1985, p. 113.   2. *Time,* March 4, 1985, p. 75.   3. *Rocky*

Mountain News, January 14, 1985, p. 2G.   4. *Rolling Stone*, Summer 1986, p. 121.   5. *People*, May 13, 1985, p. 43.   6. *People*, March 11, 1985, p. 116. 7. *Spin*, April 1986, p. 54.

JOHN COUGAR MELLENCAMP

It's a long way from sadomasochism to patriotism, but John Cougar Mellencamp covers that entire lyrical spectrum. One of his earliest hits was "Hurts So Good," in which he invited his lover to sink her teeth into his bones and make it "hurt so good." Three years later he endeared himself to the nation with his sweet, nostalgic "Small Town."

After experiencing the altruism of Live Aid, John Cougar Mellencamp departed from some of his earlier, more rebellious attitudes. Several years ago during a London, Ontario, concert in front of fourteen thousand fans, he launched into an obscenity-laced tirade against the concert's promoters, flung rented equipment into the packed audience, allegedly injuring two women, and walked offstage.[1]

Mellencamp declared, "I swear because I know it's not socially acceptable, so I do it around people I know are going to be upset. I hate things that are this-is-the-way-you-are-supposed-to-behave. That why I hate schools, governments, and churches."[2] His popular "Jack and Diane" was an anthem of youthful rebellion. The "Authority Song" was in the same vein, though both songs lacked the viciousness of many of the anti-authority songs of heavy metal groups.

When criticized for the video "Hurts So Good" showing women in chains, Mellencamp said, "Sex, violence, rebellion—it's all part of rock 'n' roll."[3] Now, with his tune "Small Town" joining "Pink Houses" as populist anthems, Mellencamp says, "I've never voted, I've never registered to vote, but I will this time."[4] Mellencamp, who is dropping the name Cougar, seems to be maturing, certainly a welcome sign for the late eighties.

1. *Rolling Stone*, October 28, 1982, p. 39.   2. *People*, October 11, 1982. 3. *Musician*, February 1983, p. 22.   4. *Rolling Stone*, (no date), John Cougar Mellencamp interview.

MOTLEY CRUE

Their first commercial hit album featured a black front emblazoned with a satanic pentagram. It was entitled, *Shout at the Devil*. Critics accused them of devilish overtones. Bass player Nikki Sixx defended the group by saying, "We're about as anti-Satan as you can get. We're trying to say that the devil is any authority who tells you what you can do and what you can't do. It can be your parents, it can be your teachers, it can be your boss. We're saying shout at the f------. Don't let them get you down!"[1]

Critics were even more alarmed when Sixx said, "We're the loudest, grossest band in the history of rock 'n' roll. Motley Crue isn't just a name. It's an image, and we do our damnedest to live up to it at all times."[2]

Tunes like "Red Hot" describe "love from a shotgun, licensed to kill." Another tune called "Bastard" extols the virtues of oral sex. Crue's lipstick and war paint, outrageously long hairstyles, knee boots, and skinny top-to-bottom black leather and studs appealed to heavy metal fans. Their tour bus featured a sex room in the back, outfitted to show pornographic videotapes. An article in a rock periodical claimed they took one young woman onto the bus and inflicted sadomasochistic sex acts upon her. Sixx says, "We treat women like s---. We're not Boy Scouts."[3] Sixx also said, "The only thing I care about is rock 'n' roll, chicks, and my bottle of Jack Daniels."[4]

Vince Neal of the band was charged with vehicular manslaughter after a drunk driving incident that killed his passenger, a member of the rock group Hanoi Rocks. The automobile Neal collided with carried two passengers, and both were seriously injured. Neal received a fine and a short jail sentence. Afterwards, Nikki Sixx said, "We're not here to endorse sobriety, but we're definitely not here to endorse being complete drunks either."[5]

Their album *Theater of Pain* contained songs like "City Boy Blues," in which the singer says, "Don't look to Jesus to change your seasons." In the tune "Fight for Your Rights" the singer asks, "Who wrote the Bible?" He adds, "Save our souls for a life so good it sure feels bad."

Nick Mars of the band, a Baptist minister's son who was born in Huntington, Indiana, says, "I'm just as sick as the others, although I prefer to do my sickness in private."[6]

For those who thought Crue might mellow, Nikki Sixx scuttled such hope by saying, "We're the nastiest, sleaziest band that's ever come down the pike, and we're proud of that. We have no intentions of changing."[7] The band took a year-long break in 1986 but came back to record the album *Girls, Girls, Girls,* a tribute to the band's fondness for strip clubs. Describing the album, Nikki Sixx said, "It's VD rock—it's raunchier than anything we've ever done. Our attitude this time is just to pull your pants down and party."[8] Admitting the band's sexual inclinations, Sixx said, "If the Rolling Stones had started in 1980, this is what it would sound like, real street, real raunch, right from the crotch."[9] One can only wonder when the words of Isaiah 59:12 might catch up with them: "Our transgressions are multiplied before us. Our sins testify against us."

1. *Hit Parader,* December 1983, pp. 36-37.   2. Ibid.   3. *Circus,* May 31, 1984, p. 48.   4. *Hit Parader,* August 1984, pp. 20-22.   5. *Circus,* April 30, 1986, p. 59. 6. *Circus,* November 30, 1985, p. 84.   7. *Hit Parader,* May 1985, p. 6.   8. *Hit Parader,* May 1987, p. 40.   9. *Circus,* March 31, 1987, p. 42.

STEVIE NICKS

Before each concert, the backstage dressing rooms of Fleetwood Mac are stocked with spareribs, fresh limes, Blue Nun white wine, cognac, and bottles of Dom Perignon.[1] Their contracts demand such symbols of rock power. "You can go your own way," they once declared to Mac fans, and each group member has done just that: bass guitarist John McVie to a drug bust in his Hawaiian paradise home; Mick Fleetwood to Ghana, Africa, to record budding native musicians; and Stevie Nicks, Christine McVie, and Lindsey Buckingham to solo careers. Stevie Nicks has also ventured into intense exploration of the occult.

Stevie admits believing in spirits, confesses that Halloween is her favorite night of the year, dabbles in reincarnation philosophy, wants to talk to a ghost, and expresses a desire to build her own pyramid and live in a witch-house.

The idea for the cover of her solo album *Bella Donna* came to her in a dream. It features a crystal ball (endorsing divination), a tambourine (symbolizing the porthole of perception to the spirit world), and three roses (representing the power of pyramids).[2]

The *Bella Donna* album credits list Maya Design studios for clothing assistance. Maya is a name for the Hindu goddess Devi, who represents the illusory nature of the material world. Bella Donna is also the name of a powerful poison, an interesting word choice that forewarns in the title cut, "Bella Donna . . . sort of captures your soul." No wonder *Rolling Stone* called her "Fleetwood Mac's blond priestess of the occult."[3]

1. *The Vancouver Sun,* December 27, 1979, p. 6.   2. *Rolling Stone,* September 3, 1981, p. 18.   3. *Rolling Stone,* September 17, 1981, p. 57.

TED NUGENT

Billing himself as "the guitar gunslinger," Ted Nugent makes no
attempt to placate those seeking sophisticated pop music. He calls
his music "combat rock," which involves a barrage of feedback and
stage acrobatics, including Nugent's leap from atop amplifiers clad
only in a loincloth. His pornographic lyrics are accompanied by
guitar riffs amplified beyond the threshold of pain. Nugent performs
with earplugs but allows no such protection for his audiences.
Describing his outlook on rock, he declares, "Rock is a perfect
primal method of releasing our violent instincts. I used to rape [an
audience]. Now I like a little foreplay. I literally demand a reaction
from an audience."[1] He apparently gets what he wants. As rock's
ignoble savage, Ted easily maintains his image as the Motor City
Madman.

1. *Circus,* May 13, 1976, p. 29.

OZZY OSBOURNE

After a decade of service to Black Sabbath, Ozzy Osbourne, the
diabolical former lead singer for England's heavy metal Satan-
rockers, is on his own. Lest anyone think that his split with Sabbath
bodes good, Ozzy warns, "I'm just as evil and just as crazy as
ever."[1]

No one who was there when he bit the head off a live dove at a
CBS executive meeting would doubt him. "I wanted them to
remember me," he explains, describing how he spat the remains on
the table.[2] There's a lot to remember about Ozzy. Though he
acknowledges the Satan-worshiping image in Sabbath's early days
was a marketing ploy, he clings to his fascination with Lucifer. He
professes a belief in future and past existences, one of which was
lived as a "servant of the devil."[3] He is fascinated with Aleister
Crowley, the famous British spiritualist, whom Ozzy calls "a
phenomenon of his time."[4]

Drugs seemed as much a part of his life as the devil. He admits
taking LSD every day for years, spending a thousand dollars a week
on dope, snorting cocaine "by the bagful," and sampling heroin.[5]
Opposed to hard drug usage, he states, "I can't say that I knock
drugs. When you're having fun it's great, but when someone has to
pay for it, it's bad."[6]

His album *Diary of a Madman* was promoted by a $2 million

concert tour featuring special effects and macabre props, including gallons of pig's blood.[7] A printed release enclosed with the LP publicized Ozzy's feelings: "I have become infatuated with the feeling of horror. . . . If my ideas seem disordered in intellect or slightly psychotic . . . it is because they are." Ozzy argues rather unconvincingly, "I am not a bad person . . . or wish to harm anyone."[8]

His album *Speak of the Devil* featured a fanged Ozzy vomiting simulated human flesh. *Speak of the Devil* included an earlier Black Sabbath tune praising marijuana entitled "Sweet Leaf." The album *Diary of a Madman* featured inverted crosses and black magic hieroglyphics. The tune "Little Dolls" spoke of voodoo. After biting the head off a bat and urinating on the Alamo, fans wondered what might come next. Pig intestines and calf livers were thrown into the audience, and a midget called Little John was ceremoniously hung. A rider in Ozzy's contract specified that the concert promoter must provide "twenty-five pounds of calf livers and pig's intestines."

A certified schizophrenic who has attempted suicide, Ozzy admits that at age eleven he stabbed his aunt's cat.[9] He wanted to build a black cathedral in his backyard with magic circles and a hexagonal roof.[10] Defending his image, Ozzy claimed to be a Christian and said, "God is within you. God is nice feelings. A Christian is a man who is within himself who puts out good vibes. I'm not a maniac devil worshiper. I'm just playing a role I have fun with. I want people to think I'm wild because they get a kick out of it."[11]

He defends his support of Aleister Crowley by saying, "It's done to be theatrical. You can sing about Crowley and present a good stage show without being the devil."[12] His album *The Ultimate Sin* was criticized for demonic overtones. Ozzy explained, "It's whatever you want it to be. There are different sins to different people. . . . Right now, I'd have to say the ultimate sin is the threat of nuclear war."[13]

Ozzy admits his stint in the Betty Ford Center for Drug Abuse helped. Of his prior drug usage, he says, "If it wasn't a sniff of cocaine, it was a pill. If it wasn't a pill, it was a smoke of dope. If it wasn't dope, it was a bottle of booze." Ozzy married his manager, who bore him two children, and he settled down somewhat. He claimed to be a family man but admitted his two-year-old daughter had picked up her father's affinity for four-letter sex verbs. Though bowed by his bout with alcoholism, Ozzy wanted the public to know he wasn't beaten. He declared, "This doesn't mean I'm going to become some born-again Christian. . . . I'm not going to tell other people not to drink."[14] In a 1987 interview, Ozzy seems to have mellowed slightly. Though he had no definite plans to retire from the rock scene, he claims to have an interest in his family life, something he could not pursue with a full-time touring career.[15]

1. *Hit Parader*, March 1981, p. 27.   2. *Rolling Stone*, May 14, 1981, p. 41.
3. *Circus*, August 26, 1980, p. 26.   4. Ibid.   5. *People*, September 7, 1981.
6. *Circus*, June 30, 1981, p. 39.   7. *Rolling Stone*, November 12, 1981, p. 39.
8. *Circus*, August 26, 1980, p. 26.   9. *Hit Parader*, June 1982, p. 29.   10. *Circus*, March 31, 1983, p. 45.   11. *US*, May 21, 1984, p. 38.   12. *Hit Parader*, February 1984, p. 14.   13. *Hit Parader*, August 1985, p. 20.   14. *Circus*, April 30, 1985, p. 99.   15. *Hit Parader*, May 1987, p. 60.

PINK FLOYD**

With forty-foot helium-inflated pigs floating in the air, a fusillade of fireworks, the amplified sounds of someone walking on the ceiling, a 35' x 210' cardboard wall rising from the stage, Pink Floyd concerts were rock theater at its best—or worst, depending on one's moral perspective. Their avant-garde sounds, propelled by the sale of 6.5 million units of their 1973 release *Dark Side of the Moon*, blitzed drug-doped audiences with high-tech space-rock sound.

This British group had its genesis in the 1960s under the tutelage of the acid-experimenting genius of Syd Barrett. His psychedelic inclinations introduced the group to sight and sound effects that accompanied tunes like "Chapter 24" (a musical adaptation of the occult I Ching). Barrett, who quit the group, was left behind for the Pinkies' space-rock voyage of the 1980s.

One album, *The Wall*, earned Pink Floyd an amazing $20 million in one year by topping the charts week after week. *The Wall* chronicled the emotional torment of a successful rock star (Roger Waters, writer of the lyrics and music) who builds up a "wall" of defenses against an absent father, a smothering mother, and a sadistic schoolmaster.

The Wall lyrics explored psychic powers ("Nobody Home"), sex ("Young Lust"—"I need a dirty woman"), and educational anarchism. In "Another Brick in the Wall," Pink Floyd caustically intones that youth "don't need no education" or "thought control."

What high school teacher could cope with students who heeded the plea: "Hey, teacher, leave them kids alone!'"?

ELVIS PRESLEY**

The bizarre stage antics of today's rock groups are possible because one man destroyed the moral barriers constraining public entertainment. Known for his gyrating pelvis and lewd gestures, that man was Elvis Presley. So great was the influence of "the King" that fans marched on Washington after his death to insist his birthday be declared a national holiday. But "the King" had his problems. Various magazines quoted friends and confidants that Elvis was addicted to a variety of drugs, including heroin. A bodyguard claimed Elvis's buttocks were so pocked with needle marks there was little room left for injections. The man who fervently sang "He Touched Me" and "How Great Thou Art" finally became unable to eat, sleep, or sing without the aid of pills.

Some claimed Elvis harbored a morose interest in the occult. He studied paranormal phenomena and communicated regularly with a psychic in Denver, Colorado. Elvis claimed he could form clouds with the power of his mind and would sometimes load friends into his limousine for a midnight visit to the coroner or the graveyard. One intimate friend said Elvis believed he was Jesus, with the power to draw out diseases by his hands.

From a $35-a-week truck driver to a singer with an amassed career income of $4.3 billion, Elvis captured the heart of America like no other popular entertainer before or since. On the way, he turned from an Assembly of God choirboy into a devotee of the Hindu mystic Paramahansa Yogananda, founder of the Self-Realization Fellowship. Though some prominent preachers insisted Elvis made it to heaven, the only certainty was that calories and chemicals ended a career unparalleled in entertainment history.

THE PRETENDERS

Leather-love songs of violent amatory experiences might be expected from Judas Priest and Scorpion, but Chrissie Hynde of the Pretenders is a woman. That doesn't seem to deter her. In "Tattooed Love Boys," she describes a quasi-rape scene in which a lover treats her so roughly that a plastic surgeon must patch things up. Sex to Chrissie may mean that lust not only "turns to anger" but also transforms "a kiss to a slug." "Up the Neck" records her emotions after one such encounter. "Bad Boys Get Spanked" turns the tables, complete with whacking sounds, groans, and screams. In "Brass in Pocket" she plans to vary normal lovemaking by inventively using her "imagination" as well as her "arms . . . legs . . . fingers . . . style."

With ripped jeans, crinkled leather jacket, and disheveled hair, Chrissie evokes the consummate punk gang look. Forsaking femininity, she exudes toughness. She boasts, "Every night I get some girl coming backstage who says to me that halfway through the set she forgot I was a girl!"[1] Her coaxing vulgarity and street language accompany a cultivated interest in palmistry, numerology, and black magic. The boys in the band also reflect her wayward ways. Guitarist James Honeyman-Scott acknowledged an addiction to speed, acute alcoholic cirrhosis of the liver, and a proclivity for cocaine—and died of an overdose.

Chrissie Hynde, a vegetarian and devout believer in reincarnation, regularly visits a Krishna temple near her London home.[3] But such devotion to passive religious principles contradicts her comment during one concert. She advised the audience to "throw petrol bombs at your [shopping] malls."[4]

1. *Circus,* October 31, 1981, p. 25.   2. *Rolling Stone,* May 20, 1980, p. 29.
3. *People,* April 23, 1987.   4. *Rolling Stone,* March 26, 1987, p. 34.

PRINCE

Called Prince after his father's stage name, his full name is Prince Rogers Nelson. One of the more talented and versatile black musicians ever to enter pop music, he initially appealed to homosexuals with a scantily-clad image and lyrics endorsing incest and homosexual oral sex.

His tune "Darling Nikki" stirred a national protest over pornographic lyrics. It described a nymphomaniacal girl sitting in a hotel lobby "masturbating with a magazine." In the tune "Head," he told of a bride who meets him on her way to be wed. She engages in oral sex to preserve her virginity. *Rolling Stone* magazine described his quest for fame as a belief in "humanism through hedonism, social freedom through sexual anarchy."[1] In the title cut of the album

Controversy, he depicted a sexual act, then recited the Lord's Prayer. At the climax of stage performances featuring the album, he raised his arms in a mock crucifixion before a lighted cross. Other stage antics included simulated intercourse in a bed and a shower in a tub. The movie *Purple Rain* ended with Prince stroking the neck of his guitar, simulating masturbation until seminal fluid squirted from its end. The soundtrack album from that film sold 8.8 million copies.

All of his albums contain liner notes giving thanks to God, but *People* magazine observed, "The gospel he preaches is salvation by sex."[2] Other religious themes include a line from the tune "Darling Nikki"—"I'm fine because the Lord is coming soon." He admits his father beat his mother, who kept pornographic books and sexual vibrators in her room.[3] Prince shuns liquor and drugs and once left an open Bible in a band member's hotel room with a Scripture noted. One periodical said of him, "On stage he was the erotic Pope of Pop, possessed by his passion play. . . . He'd wail in falsetto and perform coital contortions with a brass bed when necessary. Comparing Michael Jackson to Prince is like comparing Peter Pan with the Marquis de Sade."[4]

The album *Around the World in a Day* contained a sensual song called "Temptation." Prince described his body as a "hot flash of animal lust." Toward the end of the song, he mocks God, who declares to Prince, "You have to want it for the right reasons. You don't, now you die."

His first big pop hit, "Little Red Corvette," contained references to condoms. Such crass eroticism coupled with spiritual overtones profoundly disturbed a critic writing in *Newsweek.* He described Prince singing the song "I Would Die for You," in which Prince declares, "I'm your messiah." The writer told of twelve thousand adoring fans and said, "It was a very creepy experience [with] morbid implications. . . . Watching it happen, it is hard not to wonder where Prince is heading and just how far his millions of fans will follow."[5]

Prince's song "Sexuality" declares that a second coming, a "New-Age revolution," is on the horizon, an era when "anything goes." Where would Prince go next? His self-indulgent movie *Under the Cherry Moon* bombed, although his video for the tune "Kiss," showing Prince simulating copulation, was an instant success. His album *Sign o' the Times* shot to the top of the charts using his proven formula of eroticism and religion. Songs on the album range from

"The Cross" ("Don't die without knowing the cross") to "It" ("I want to do it . . . in a bed, on the stairs, anywhere").

As a maniacal messiah, Prince is a rock force to be reckoned with. Although he and his band, the Revolution, pray backstage before each show, one insider who worked with him says, "He wants to control people through his pathological paranoid personality."[6] With oblique lyrics about God and explicit lyrics about sex, perhaps Prince should listen to the lyrics in his song, "The Ladder": "Everyone wants salvation of the soul."

1. *Rolling Stone*, December 9, 1982, p. 67.   2. *People*, November 19, 1984, p. 161. 3. Ibid., p. 162.   4. *US*, September 10, 1984, p. 44.   5. *Newsweek*, April 29, 1985.   6. Ibid.

QUEEN

"We want to shock and be outrageous," says lead singer, Freddie Mercury.[1] Their name with its gay-drag connotation is appropriate. Queen lyrics range from the unprintable sex solicitation of "Get Down, Make Love" to the blasphemous chorus, "All going down to see the Lord Jesus." Their LP *Jazz* was promoted by Queen's sponsorship of a nude bicycle race that featured fifty-five undraped entrants. For two hours, Mercury whips concert audiences into a frenzy with erotic body contortions. Little wonder that their song, "We Are the Champions," has been widely accepted as a gay liberation anthem. "On stage, I am a devil," Freddie brags. "I think I may go mad in several years' time."[2]

From their crest of animals, representing the astrological signs of each member, to their tours, among rock's most lavish and expensive, Queen spares nothing to maintain its image as one of the music business's most bizarre acts. Their tours have featured snake charmers, strippers, transvestites, and a naked lady who smokes cigarettes between her legs. Though lead singer Freddie Mercury encourages a debauched public image, he is rivaled by his colleague, drummer Roger Taylor, who admits, "I like strippers and wild parties with naked women. I'd love to own a whorehouse. What a wonderful way to make a living."[3]

The group insists it's all contrived to attract crowds, but illusion and reality affect both a culture's values and the morals of teen record buyers, who only see Queen's pornographic parodies.

Queen's popularity showed signs of waning in the mid-1980s. The

1986 album *A Kind of Magic* did poorly, in spite of a clever video for
the title song.

Queen is probably among the more talented of contemporary
rock groups, and some of their earlier albums, notably the innova-
tive *A Night at the Opera,* show that rock does not have to be inferior
musically. Freddie Mercury is a competent pianist, and Brian May
is regarded as a top-notch guitarist. Mercury and May have written
some clever songs, many of them not offensive at all. It is regret-
table that talented musicians and songwriters feel compelled to
maintain bizarre and immoral life-styles to keep audiences interested.

1. *Circus,* April 1974, p. 41.   2. Ibid., March 17, 1977, p. 42.   3. *Rolling Stone,*
June 11, 1981, p. 46.

RATT

Ratt described their concert series as a "world infestation tour," an
apt image for this Los Angeles-based quintet. An early album
featured a dozen live rats crawling up a girl's leg. An advertisement
for the album *Out of the Cellar* declared, "They're out of the cellar
and out to conquer the earth." Stephen Pearcy of the group says,
"We like sex, and we like getting loose after a show."[1]

The destination sign above the windshield of their travel bus
invites women to expose their breasts. One magazine described
their touring vehicle as a "rolling Sodom and Gomorrah," a "nightmare vision of rock depravity."[2]

Robbin Crosby of the band says, "I don't have a love life, I have a
lust life."[3] The hedonist hymns "Sweet Cheater" and "Back for
More" bear lyrical testimony to Ratt's intentions. The video for "Lay
It Down" suggests prepubescent sex between two youngsters at a
birthday party. Their libidinous lyrics are matched by the devotion
of their fans, postpubescents whose attention spans seem limited to
the hormonal moment and who frequently throw panties and bras on
stage.

Interestingly, Ratt's 1986 album has the title *Life's a Bitch.* For a
group that seems to pride itself on its hedonism, Ratt chose a title
that conveys the idea that life isn't pleasant after all. But don't think
that Ratt is changing direction. Most likely the title is itself a call to
pleasure-seeking. After all, if youth perceive that life is really

terrible, isn't that a reason to indulge one's appetites as much as possible?

1. *Hit Parader,* August 1985, p. 35.   2. *People,* August 12, 1985, pp. 117-119.
3. *Circus,* September 30, 1985, pp. 43-48.

THE ROLLING STONES

Though tempered by affluence, their early image of savagery, evil, and rebellion is intact, thanks to Keith Richards' heroin bust and Mick Jagger's promiscuous meanderings. Richards admits, "There are black magicians who think we are acting as unknown agents of Lucifer.[1] To support such speculation, the Stones' songs have ranged from supporting violent revolution in "Street Fighting Man" to the satanists' anthem, "Sympathy for the Devil." The death of four fans at the fateful Altamont rockfest solidified their image as purveyors of the sinister.

A Stones concert is an orgy of sexual celebration, with Jagger as head cheerleader. Strutting and prancing across the stage, his androgynous performances delight both men and women. On one tour, his playacting concluded with a giant phallic balloon rising out of the stage. "Sometimes, being on stage is better than an orgasm," Jagger claims.[2] Press reports circulate regularly that Jagger is bisexual, and one story blamed a Jagger-David Bowie relationship for breaking up the latter's marriage. True or not, such speculation is part of Mick's aura as rock's spokesman for hedonism. He admits that his first sexual experience was homosexual and wants his daughter to experience sex at an early age.[3]

The aging multimillionaires of rock continue to convey lawless outrage while cavorting with high society and seeking tax shelters. Their proclivity for sexual explicitness that shocked fans a decade ago hardly raises a blush today. A stunned public was offended when they urinated on the streets of London in the 1960s, but today their overindulgence in cocaine and sadomasochism is considered chic at best, titillating at worst.

Today's band members average more than forty years of age, and Bill Wyman is over fifty. Showing no signs of mellowing, the Stones' tune, "She Was Hot," describes a singer lost in a woman's "burning flesh" as she "pinned me to the ground." The tune "Too Much Blood" describes a man cutting off a woman's head, putting her body in a refrigerator, and then features the singer yelling sexual expletives.

Commenting on his promiscuity and infidelity to his live-in lover, Jerri Hall, Mick Jagger said, "I've told Jerri I can't feel cut off from half the population."[4] Jagger also said, "I'm against marriage. It's legal claptrap."[5] (Jagger did eventually marry Hall.) As for sex, he says, "We all want to have an affair with our mother."[6]

He once declared he'd rather die than sing "Satisfaction" at age thirty. As he and the other Stones continue to rock on (their 1981 tour grossed an estimated $127 million, including $300,000 a day on T-shirt sales alone), Jagger's sadomasochistic view of women lingers with salacious lines like, "When the whip comes down," and "Am I rough enough?" (from "Beast of Burden").

Simple sex hasn't been abandoned. "Emotional Rescue" found Jagger lamenting that he was hot for a girl who was "so cold" that she had an "Arctic soul." He warned her that, when she got old, nobody would care that she had been a "sweet, sweet virgin." *Tattoo You* continued in the Stones sexist tradition with tunes like "Little T & A" and "Start Me Up," in which Jagger complains about his lover's violent lovemaking manners of "roughing it up" by commenting, "You make a grown man cry."

Jagger's Luciferian bent found competition in guitarist Keith Richards, whose heroin bust highlighted his ten-year habit. Former associate Tony Sanchez charged in a book entitled *Up and Down with the Rolling Stones* that Richards underwent a total blood-exchange transfusion for a 1975 tour to pass U.S. immigration officials. Sanchez also accuses Richards and his common-law wife, Anita Pallenberg, with sojourns into black magic, bisexuality, and turning children on to heroin and cocaine.[7] He also claims that Richards' drug habit ran to a thousand dollars a day. In Tony's words, the Stones are "the loneliest men I have ever known."[8]

Reportedly clean of smack now, Richards speaks candidly of his flirtation with addictive drugs: "I don't regret what I did. Everybody needs a little kick of something. . . ."[9] Mick Jagger condones cocaine use by declaring, "If you want to take it, fine . . . what a boring drug."[10]

The Stones are worshiped with messianic adulation. Jagger does nothing to dispel the image, singing in "Emotional Rescue" that he wants to be "your savior . . . steadfast and true." But *Newsweek* called the Stones' 1980s music an "erotic exorcism for a doomed decade."[11]

Keith Richards once observed that Stones' songs come spontaneously, like inspiration "at a seance." He explains that the tunes
arrive "en masse," as if the Stones were only a willing "medium."[12]
With voodoo incantations and the screams of demon possession
accompanying cuts like "Dancing with Mr. D" (the devil), its
questionable if the satanic imagery of Mr. Jagger and company is
simple creativity. One thing is certain: Their fans aren't the only
victims. As Jagger expresses the frustrations of stardom and sensual
satiation in their hit, "Shattered," he concludes that fame and
fortune have left him in tatters. After working to achieve "success
and sex," he asks, "Does it matter?" A tongue-in-cheek advertisement for their album *Dirty Work* declared, "clean hands, pure minds,
dirty work." They should be sued for false advertising. There's
nothing pure about this band, especially their minds.

1. *Rolling Stone,* August 19, 1971.   2. *Rolling Stone,* July 17, 1975, p. 37.
3. *People,* October 3, 1977, p. 108.   4. *USA Today,* January 30, 1985, p. 2D.
5. *Rolling Stone,* January 20, 1983, p. 28.   6. Ibid.   7. *Newsweek,* September 17,
1979, p. 95.   8. *Circus,* December 11, 1979, p. 35.   9. *US,* November 10, 1981,
p. 29.   10. *Rolling Stone,* May 29, 1980, p. 34.   11. *Newsweek,* October 5, 1981,
p. 61.   12. *Rolling Stone,* May 5, 1977, p. 55.

SCORPIONS

The first German heavy metal band to gain worldwide recognition,
the Scorpions called themselves "virgin killers." The album with
that name showed the photo of a naked ten-year-old girl sitting on
shards of jagged glass, her legs spread open and arrows pointing to
her genitals. Their big Top Forty hit was entitled, "Rock You Like a
Hurricane." The singer says his lover is hungry, so he is going to
"give her inches and feed her well."

Klaus Mien of the band says the song is autobiographical. "It's
strange waking up in some strange city with a new girl lying next to
you every day, but it's something we've gotten used to," Mien
declares.[1] Complaints were registered about the album, *Love at First
Sting,* from which the tune "Rock You like a Hurricane" was taken.
The cover depicted a partially clad couple embracing, as the man
tattooed a scorpion on the woman's thigh. More offensive was the
cover for the album *Black Out,* which showed a lobotomy patient
whose eyes were being clawed out by bent forks. The album *Animal
Magnetism* pictured a woman kneeling in front of a man's legs as a
Doberman pinscher thrust out its tongue.[2] In response to cries of
protest, a member of the band said, "It was a sensual cover.

. . . Rock 'n' roll is a very sensual form, and we're a very sensual band."[3]

1. *Hit Parader,* May 1984, p. 21.   2. *Circus,* October 31, 1985, p. 56.   3. *Hit Parader,* January 1984, p. 6.

BRUCE SPRINGSTEEN

Springsteen is to the 1980s what Dylan was to the 1960s, and he has been compared to Elvis and Jagger. He is rock's national troubadour, a modern Woody Guthrie, and an energetic entertainer whose four-hour concerts exhilarate fans. When his album *Born to Run* hit the charts in the mid-1970s, *Newsweek* and *Time* proclaimed him the now-and-future superstar.

Springsteen started in barroom bands on New Jersey's summer shores. Columnist George Will wrote, "There is a message in many of his songs. It's an affirmation that life is hard, but not bad because it's hard."[1]

With the E Street Band, he produces one of the most emotional shows ever witnessed in rock 'n' roll. Springsteen leaps onto amps, tumbles into crowds, and vocalizes with frenetic abandon. The hard edge of his music evokes images of the cars, bikes, and concrete scenes of his native New Jersey.

His 1985 nationwide tour took him before 5 million fans in eleven countries, earned $90 million in tickets, and sold out 152 concerts—the biggest tour in rock history.

Novelist Bobbie Ann Mason analyzed the Springsteen success: "There's nothing but joy and good feeling in his music, and he speaks for the dark side of people's feelings at the same time."[2]

Springsteen has been called the Rambo of rock 'n' roll and spokesperson for a new patriotism. His hit song "Born in the USA" became a 1980s anthem. His album *Bruce Springsteen and the E Street Band Live/1975-85* catapulted him to financial prosperity few performers dream of. The five-LP package debuted at the Number One spot on the charts, a status achieved by only one other album, and was expected to earn $450 million.

Unlike many rock stars who collect groupies and trash hotel rooms, Springsteen is married and socially mature. He donates heavily to shelters for the homeless and food banks, and frequently sings about the unemployed. His song "Seeds" details the plight of a man who leaves the dust bowl for the streets of Houston.

Love is summed up in his offhand reference to Mary, a girl he got pregnant ("Thunder Road"), and lust of life is epitomized by the "stolen car" he drives down Elridge Avenue (from *The River* album). Combining sex with the biker's philosophy, Springsteen declares, "Just wrap your legs around these velvet rims and strap your hands across my engines." In the tune "Fourth of July, Asbury Park" he describes factory girls underneath the boardwalk who promise to "unsnap their jeans."

Springsteen laments the spiritual emptiness of the Asbury waste-land by saying, "When I was growing up, the only thing that never let me down was rock 'n' roll."[3] As one secular rock critic put it, "Upon this rock [the statement just quoted] Springsteen has built his church."[4]

An excellent description of Bruce Springsteen's universal appeal to the masses was found in a *Rolling Stone* editorial analyzing his popularity as Artist of the Year: "In the public's eye, he is both easygoing and fiercely inspiring, both an ordinary working-class guy and a multimillionaire. He inspires millions of fans to feel an intense personal relationship with him, but he is, in fact, isolated and remote. He is rarely seen in public, virtually never speaks to the media, and releases albums infrequently. He is both a rebel and a patriot, claimed by the political left and right. He is life-size and larger than life."[5]

Less offensive than most artists with his Americana perspective ("My Home Town"), one still wonders about fans' adulation of an entertainer who uses God's name in vain and introduces "This Land Is Your Land" as an alternative to "God Bless America."

1. *USA Today,* November 14, 1986, p. 2A. 2. Ibid. 3. *Time,* August 7, 1978, p. 73. 4. Ibid. 5. *Rolling Stone,* February 26, 1987, p. 10.

ROD STEWART

Mention Rod Stewart and the average rock fan thinks of Rod's love life as much as his music. The latter has been heavily laden with erotic overtones from "Tonight's the Night," in which he requests his angel to "spread" her wings so he can "come inside," to "Hot Legs" ("keep my pencil sharp"). His first big hit, "Maggie May," was addressed to a lover who wrecked his bed after she "wore him out."

When questioned about his heavy cosmetics and fey performances, he says, "I always wanted to be attractive to men. That's half the people who buy our records."[1] In real life, Stewart has been linked with a bevy of luscious women, though he concedes he takes Vitamin E to keep up with his rapacious sex life. "A happy home life, security, and in-laws aren't conducive to making rock 'n' roll," he stated.[2] Succeeding where Britt Ekland failed, a pregnant Alana Hamilton finally married him, but Rod soon proved unfaithful and a lengthy divorce proceeding followed. Rod Stewart proved that sex sells records and that an artist's reputation for fornication can maintain stardom as much as the musical efforts that brought notoriety.

1. *Rolling Stone,* June 21, 1973, p. 39.　　2. *Circus,* October 17, 1978, p. 36.

STING

After years of mega-hits with the Police, Sting split off on his own. Outspoken and highly visible, Sting has been interviewed frequently. He declared to one magazine, "I've got everything a man could want—a beautiful home, a beautiful girlfriend, wonderful children, and money to enjoy life, and yet there's something missing."[1]

Does Sting plan to marry and legitimize the birth of his daughter, Michele? Sting says, "I don't see the point. One can procreate without the dreaded ritual."[2] A politically leftist slant tainted the tunes of his album, *The Dream of the Blue Turtles.* Sting insisted the Russians and Americans are equally untrustworthy, musing, "I hope the Russians love their children, too."

What is next for Sting? Of his past he says, "I've tried drugs, I've tried having sex with every woman who came into the room—all that stuff—and none of it seemed to satisfy me."[3] Deeply involved in the occult, one of his close friends is a clairvoyant. He says he can predict events through playing cards and that his London home is haunted. He claims he once walked into his baby daughter's room and saw all of her toy mobiles inexplicably whirling madly.[4] Two weeks later, he saw two spirits in the room and says the atmosphere turned icy cold. A spiritualist confirmed the beings and offered to expel them, but Sting and his live-in lover turned down the offer.[5] Christians must wonder what forces will guide the talented Sting in the future.

1. *US,* December 31, 1984, p. 39.　　2. Ibid.　　3. *People,* January 20, 1986, p. 100.　　4. *Newsweek,* September 30, 1985, p. 70.　　5. *Rolling Stone,* (no date).

TWISTED SISTER

"I'm a dirtbag, and I'm not ashamed of it," says lead singer Dee Snyder of Twisted Sister.[1] When the group first started performing, band members wore dresses on stage to get attention. Snyder says, "Our philosophy has always been to do anything to become famous."[2]

The lyrics to "We're Not Gonna Take It Anymore" foster rebellion. The video accompanying the tune features a dictatorial father who doesn't want his son playing the guitar to a Twisted Sister record. The opening chords of the song literally blow the boy's father through the window.

The video for the song "I Want to Rock" is set in a school where a boy chases his tyrannical teacher through the school until the instructor gets blown up. On the cover to their introductory album *Stay Hungry,* Dee Snyder holds what appears to be a human shank bone with flesh drooping from it.

After the obscurity of a Long Island rock club, Snyder now has the attention of the popular press and says of the music he plays, "Heavy metal is the only form of music other than punk that has retained the basic elements of rock 'n' roll—rebellion. Twisted Sister is the Dirty Harry of rock. We're doing terrible things but for the right side and the right reason."[3] Instead of a fan club, Twisted Sister has what it calls an "SMF friends of Twisted Sister" (SMF stands for an obscene sexual expletive). Asked about how he prepares for a concert, Dee Snyder said, "I think about things I hate.[4]

1. *Hit Parader,* March 1986, p. 37.   2. *Hit Parader,* January 1985, p. 65.
3. *Billboard,* September 22, 1984, p. 50.   4. *Rolling Stone,* November 22, 1984, p. 64.

VAN HALEN/DAVID LEE ROTH

When a rock band describes itself as "a group of barbarians who are sweeping around the world," it's obvious their goals transcend mere musical performance.[1] Former lead singer David Lee Roth confessed, "I've managed to live out 100 percent of my fantasies with pretty women I've met on the road."[2] Gesturing with the microphone as an erect phallus between his legs, he added, "We celebrate all the sex and violence of television . . . that's Van Halen."[3] Roth's rampant sexuality made the band famous with tunes like "Hot for the Teacher," describing lustful abandon. Other tunes like "House of

Pain" zeroed in on sadomasochism. Roth sang, "She said she'd try to beat me up, but her hands are always tied."

Living up to his image, David Lee Roth has been quoted as saying, "We've indulged in every possible vice that can be counted on the road."[4] He also says, "I admire and respect women. They know their place—under me."[5]

Eddie Van Halen's ingenious guitar techniques preserved the group's popularity despite David Lee Roth's departure. One concert critic described a Van Halen performance this way: "Van Halen in concert is a musical circus of sex, drugs, and rock 'n' roll cliches piled on so thick it might take the form of high camp were it not for the screaming fans devouring every exaggerated pose. Sex is celebrated in a way that makes bike gangs look like morality squads. It elevates narrow-minded rock bombast to new lows at calculated crowd manipulation, laughing all the way to the bank."[6]

With the addition of new lead singer Sammy Hagar, Van Halen's popularity continued. Roth was only a quarter of the group, which includes bass guitarist Michael Anthony, and the Dutch-born Van Halen brothers, Edward and Alex. Edward declares, "I'm in rock 'n' roll because I don't like being told what to do."[7] But Roth's high-leaping, crotch-thrusting antics defined the group's philosophy beyond realistic doubt. He proclaimed, "Whatever your vice, whatever your sexual ideas . . . whatever somebody else can't do in his nine-to-five job, I can do in rock and roll. . . . I'm in the job to exercise my sexual fantasies. When I'm onstage, it's like doing it with 20,000 of your closest friends. . . . I'm proud of the way we live."[8]

Their first album release with Hagar, *5150,* was the band's first Number One record. On his own, Roth has declared himself the cheerleader for "the immoral majority." Roth released an album entitled *Eat 'Em and Smile,* depicting the loudmouthed legend as a cannibal. His sexism continues in songs like "Bump and Grind" and "I'm Easy," which declares, "Come get me baby while I'm hot, hurry . . . you can have a lot."

Roth's hedonism encouraged him to suggest that Lloyd's of London offer paternity insurance for rock stars.[9] With tunes like "Feel Your Love Tonight," "Running with the Devil," "Everybody Wants Some," and "I'm Your Ice Cream Man" ("my flavor's guaranteed to satisfy") to their credit, Van Halen probably needs it. At least they give fair warning before assaulting their audience with debauchery and decibels. "Women and Children First," says one of their album titles.

1. *Circus,* October 10, 1978, p. 26.   2. *Circus,* November 14, 1979, p. 42.
3. *Circus,* October 17, 1978, p. 39.   4. *Hit Parader,* September 1982, p. 5.   5. *Hit Parader,* August 1985, p. 17.   6. *Calgary Herald,* April 28, 1984.   7. *Circus,* May 13, 1980, p. 23.   8. *Rolling Stone,* September 4, 1980, pp. 9-10, 21.   9. *People,* October 17, 1981, p. 12.

WASP

"I'm a liar and I'm a cheat, I have no morals and I'm a thief, I'm a tormentor, I'm a sadist that whips the flesh."

Those words from the song "Tormentor" are an apt description of WASP bandleader Blackie Lawless. The band's acronym stands for "We Are Sexual Perverts."[1] Song titles run the gamut from "The Torture Never Stops" and "Love Machine" to "On Your Knees," an overt description of oral sex.

Lawless claims he has been heavily influenced by the occult. About performing with his prior group, Sisters, Lawless says, "We were the first band ever to use a pentagram on a logo."[2]

WASP's early stage shows featured naked women on torture racks, whips, raw meat thrown into the audience, and blood drunk from a skull. Such antics were eventually discarded in favor of a Lawless costume with holes in the back of his pants and a buzz saw jutting from a codpiece on his crotch. Explaining such stage tactics, Lawless said, "We knew that we'd have to be totally off the wall in our appearance and sound for anyone to give us a second look. We started coming out with the most outrageous costumes we could think of."[3] With abandoned bluntness, Lawless says, "If I wasn't in WASP, I'd be out stealing cars."[4]

Later stage shows did away with the psychodramatic trappings but not the sexually explicit lyrics, as evidenced in tunes like "Ball Crusher" and "Sex Drive." The cover for the single record "Ball Crusher" shows a girl with her hand coming out of a guy's pants and holding a bloody baseball. Lawless says about attempts to censor his songs, "I don't see anything wrong with sex and violence, as long as violence is presented in a very theatrical way. It's very therapeutic for kids."[5]

Blackie admits, "I studied the occult for about three years,"[6] but after dabbling in witchcraft, he concluded, "It's all bull."[7] Such assurances mean little to those familiar with the lyrics of songs like "Hellion," in which he declares, "The gods you worship are steel, at the altar of rock 'n' roll you kneel." The WASP song, "King of Sodom and Gomorrah" was honest, at least. Lawless declared that he was indeed "King of Sodom," living a life "that's hell on wheels."

The band's 1986 album *Inside the Electric Circus* featured a cover with Lawless poised behind cage bars, clad in tigerlike stripes that had been painted on his body. Like many contemporary bands, WASP seems determined to exploit man's animal nature, something no Christian should support either emotionally or financially.

1. *Circus*, January 31, 1985, p. 38.   2. Ibid., p. 56.   3. *Hit Parader*, March 1985, p. 37.   4. *Hit Parader*, May 1987, p. 25.   5. *Hit Parader*, May 1986, p. 13.
6. *Circus*, July 31, 1985, p. 90.   7. *Hit Parader*, January 1985, p. 57.

THE WHO**

The body count is in, and here are the results: Three Mile Island, Diablo Canyon, and all nuclear facilities combined—0. The Who— 11.

So why didn't protestors picket Who concerts? After all, it was Peter Townshend himself who declared in rare remorse after the fateful Cincinnati concert, "You try to convince yourself that it had nothing to do with us, but that would be a bit childish. . . . We're a big part of rock 'n' roll, so we feel partly responsible."[1]

One rock magazine commented on the tragic death of eleven Who fans, trampled by compatriots in a dope-induced, hysterical rush to be first at the foot of the stage: "Who's going to see the Who? Not Boy Scouts. Rock mega-stars must wake up. They hold sway over an entire generation. . . . There is very definitely a responsibility that goes with it."[2]

The death of drummer Keith Moon and the Cincinnati debacle did little to sober Townshend and Company. Peter declared to the press, "We had to reduce it because if we'd actually admitted to ourselves the true significance of the event [Cincinnati] . . . we could not have gone on. . . . We don't [expletive] around worrying about eleven people dying. . . . When you go on the road, you put an armor around yourself . . . you almost go into a trance."[3] This blase attitude toward violence isn't surprising. In their early days, the Who was known for setting off smoke bombs and smashing instruments to smithereens at the end of a performance. On one tour, band members inflicted $30,000 worth of damages on a Holiday Inn to celebrate the drummer's birthday. The object of festivity, Keith Moon, carried a hatchet in his luggage to chop up the furniture when he felt bored.

Violence wasn't the Who's only message. An album entitled *Face Dances* vividly described compulsive masturbatory impulses by asking, "How can you do it alone?" In "You," the lyricist described his lover as inviting his advances with open arms while her "legs are crossed."

While the Who explored the outer limits of rock's sanity, Townshend confessed, "Rock is going to kill me, somehow. It gets everybody in the end."[4] Perhaps its destructive message is best illustrated by post-Cincinnati T-shirts, stamped with footprints and the words, "I survived the Who concert."

Tommy and the Who are thought of almost simultaneously, the former being the latter's ambitious rock opera that spawned an Ann-Margret movie. Mocking Christ, *Tommy* depicted a surreal crucifixion and a vivid child molestation scene ("Lift up the night-shirt, and fiddle Uncle Ernie").

The spiritual and musical mentor of the group, Peter Townshend, was known for his wildly atavistic stage act and espousal of Eastern mysticism via the teachings of Meher Baba. Townshend mellowed with his devotion to Baba. A solo album dedicated to the guru contained songs extolling reincarnation and a tune adapted from the Baba's Hindu prayer, "Parvardigar." Peter declared, "Baba is Christ" because being a Christian is "just like being a Baba lover."[5] Once he described a frightening encounter with demonic powers. While contemplating the Hindu "Om" chant, he entered a trance state that precipitated an out-of-body experience. Townshend claims to have heard "The Niagaran roar of a billion humans screaming,"[6] quite possibly a revelation of hell's tormented.

Lead singer Roger Daltrey played the messianic lead role of *Tommy* in the film version, but his personal life-style was less than religious. He informed his wife of promiscuous dalliances while on the road, confessing, "When you're in a hotel, a pretty young lady makes life bearable."[7]

The most tragic chapter of the Who's history starred drummer Keith Moon. His craziness was well chronicled, from the human excrement in his own living room to episodes of public exposure. Once he dared death by driving a Lincoln Continental into a swimming pool. Moon reportedly took up to twenty-five amphetamines at a time, and, finally, an overdose of thirty-two anti-alcoholism tablets ended his life. He had just finished recording the group's 1978 album *Who Are You?* Had that question been answered through understanding God's purpose for his life, Moon's tragic demise may have been averted.

1. *Billboard,* December 22, 1979, p. 41.   2. *Circus,* January 22, 1980, p. 54.
3. *Rolling Stone,* June 26, 1980, p. 38.   4. *Time,* December 17, 1979, p. 94.   5. *Hit Parader,* March 3, 1972, p. 23.   6. *Rolling Stone,* December 17, 1977, pp. 55-56.
7. *People,* December 13, 1975, p. 24.